LIVE TO INSPIRE

By

Vince McKee

Published by Motivational Press, Inc.
1777 Aurora Road
Melbourne, Florida, 32935
www.MotivationalPress.com

Manufactured in the United States of America.

ISBN: 978-1-62865-300-7

Contents

Dedication

This book is dedicated to my wife Emily and daughter Maggie. You two truly are the reason for every breath I breathe and every step I take. I love our family and can't wait to watch it continue to grow!

Acknowledgments

I want to thank the Venesile family for allowing me to tell both of your inspirational stories. I would also like to thank my mother for being a lifelong fighter and never giving up hope. I would like to give my gratitude to Jennifer and Ralph Kunes, Kim, Shawna, Ron and Bernadatte along with Chuck Galeti, Cathy Wade and Vonda Ward for allowing me to tell your inspirational stories. You were all honest and I'm a better person for knowing all of you. Thank you to John King for taking the time out of your very busy schedule to write the beautiful forward. A thank you to Janet Gorman. Your faith in me is felt in my fingertips every time I write. I want to thank my mom and dad for always being there for me and my family.

Thank you to Bob and Deb Lamb, two people who have watched me grow up over the last ten years and been some of my biggest supporters and friends. The biggest thank you goes to my wife Emily for allowing me the time and solitude needed to complete this book. Another thank you needs to go to James Friguglietti for his continued guidance as I walk along this path of being an author, never knowing which way it will take me next. Last but not least, thank you to my Lord and Savior Jesus Christ; it is through your light that all work is done.

About the author

Vince McKee is a growing force in the sports literary world. His first seven books have all helped to build his credibility as a top-notch chronicler of the impact of Ohio sports. Vince is currently the Senior VP of Acquisition and Growth for NEO Sports Insiders. He is also a free lance reporter for the Medina Gazette and Cleveland Plain Dealer. Vince is an avid Cleveland sports fan and enjoys spending time with his wife Emily and daughter Maggie. He lives in North Olmsted, OH. You can follow him on Twitter at VinceTheAuthor or email him at coachvin14@yahoo.com

Foreword

By Rev. John King

Pastor, Richfield United Church of Christ

Most readers familiar with the excellent works of Vince McKee know him as a skilled sports writer. He has a knack for getting the core of a story; not merely the stats and scores, but something deeper that drives athletes. This book moves in a different direction – or maybe not. It's not about sports heroes. But it is certainly about heroes.

Sometimes I find it astonishing how moving a ball according to Newtonian physics unites cities and divides rivals, lift us up and bring us low. Of course, it's not just about a ball; it's about the drive, discipline, perseverance and yes, inspiration that make individuals into heroes. Great sports writers capture that spirit. *Live to Inspire* is mindful of this truth: there are heroes all around us. They are in arenas and stadiums. They are in hospital rooms and nursing homes. They gather in churches on military bases and under bridges.

As a minister, I've had the honor of discovering inspiration from people in the most ordinary and extraordinary circumstances. A mom and dad cradle their tiny son, born too early to survive, and question how they can move on. A gang member on the streets of El Salvador who seeks a better way. A gay couple who celebrate that they, too, have the freedom to commit their lives to one another in marriage. A dying woman, who clutches my hand as she breathes her last breath. They inspire me day by day. They both ask me - and teach me - to live to inspire.

In the years I have known Vince McKee, I have seen him to be a man of character, compassion and integrity. It comes as no surprise to me that he has seen fit to write this book. He is driven to know what inspires heroes on and off the court.

I hope that these stories inspire you as they have inspired me. These chapters moved me to tears and to smiles; they gave me courage and hope. They led me to look back and look around and notice those who have been an inspiration to me.

I hope they compel you to take notice of those people in your home and across the planet who are inspiring, yet unsung heroes. Above all, I hope they help you become the kind of person who also lives to inspire.

Rev. John King was ordained in 1988. From 1994-2004, he served the poor in El Salvador, emphasizing outreach initiatives including women's rights, literacy, street gangs, disaster relief and other social development programs. In 2010 he was credentialed for ministry in the United Church of Christ and is currently serving as pastor of Richfield UCC. He and his wife Katie live in Richfield OH with their two children.

Introduction

Why would a man who has written seven books about sports that are sold everywhere in the world and has gotten to meet almost all of his sport heroes as a kid choose to stop writing about sports and decide to take a drastic left turn? It would have had to take something truly special for me to leap from my genre of choice. In this case, like in many, things came in threes. Allow me to explain.

As I waited in line for two plus hours following an hour drive to my location, I finally had the chance to meet the one man I thought would be the centerpiece, the missing link and focal point in what would surely be my first "best seller." It was March 21, 2015, and I was standing in front of Bernie Kosar at a sports collectible store at Summit Mall in Akron. I had endured the hour long drive in typical late Cleveland bitter winter cold for the chance to meet the iconic Cleveland quarterback.

The reason for my jaunt was two prong really. I had a picture of myself and brother Don with Kosar from the 1989 NFL training camp I wanted to get signed for Don. I was 7 years old at the time and thought Kosar was the greatest thing since the extra marshmallow was added to Lucky Charms. In a way, every kid in Cleveland wanted to be Kosar at the time. Despite the fact that he had no mobility, he still made precise touchdown passes look easy and led the Browns to three AFC Championship games in the late 1980's.

Kosar had fallen on rough times recently, filing bankruptcy after several bad investments and was publicly embarrassed by being pulled over for driving under the influence. He had even been fired from his cushy job as Cleveland Browns pre-season game announcer on television. Surely such a fall from grace would have humbled the man, making him more acceptable to my upcoming request upon meeting him.

The second and even more vital reason it was necessary for me to meet Kosar that fateful day was because I had just finished my manuscript on the Browns book I had spent over two years working on. It was a great tale entitled, "Bernie, Bill and the Browns", due to be sold everywhere in August 2016. It detailed every big game, every big move and every major highlight from the time the Browns drafted Kosar to the day Art Modell moved the team to Baltimore.

It had behind the scenes interviews with some of the biggest names of that time period. The book boasted interviews with names like Reggie Langhorne, Brian Brennan, Tommy Vardell, Felix Wright, Leroy Hoard, Matt Stover, Brian Kinchen, Brian Hansen and many others. Like with any manuscript, you need to shop it around with various publishers until one makes you an offer. Despite having six previous sports books written, all of which had sold well, I was having trouble getting this one picked up. I went ahead and contacted one of the biggest sports publishers in the nation, Triumph Publishing out of Chicago. They liked the idea, but only had one issue preventing them from picking it up: the manuscript did not contain an interview with Bernie Kosar.

I told Triumph that I did everything possible to contact Kosar and he never got back to me. I had emailed him, tweeted at him, called the TV station he last appeared on; I even went as far as to call the restaurant he owns near the horse track. He never got back to me - no one got back to me - and the restaurant would reveal that he only stopped in once a month. So things looked bleak until I heard of this precious signing at the mall. I hoped it would be worth every penny of the $25 the men running the store charged you to even set foot in their line to have the chance to meet the quarterback.

I stayed up all night the evening before writing a letter to Bernie Kosar. I told him all about the book I was working on, and also how Triumph publishing refused to publish it unless I had an interview with him. I pleaded my case like any lawyer would, loaded with facts but also just the right amount of drama to make it crystal clear that this was an all or nothing situation that only he could be the savior of. I even signed a copy of each one of my previous six books to Bernie Kosar, along with having the picture printed out of when Don and I were kids with him. I figured there was no way he could possibly tell me no - I had interviewed over 50 of the biggest names in Cleveland Sports History for my prior books, and no one ever charged me for a dime or even said no. I had no reason to believe Kosar would be any different.

Surely, if men like Jim Thome, Charles Nagy, Mike Hargrove, Kenny Lofton, Carlos Baerga, Austin Carr, Larry Nance, Craig Ehlo, John Hart, Joe Tait, Len Barker, Joe Charboneua, Fred McLeod, Hector Marinaro, Otto Orf, Zoran Karic, Kenny Roda and countless others allowed me to interview them free of cost, Kosar would jump at the chance to tell his story. I mean, I even had dozens of his teammates interviewed for it.

As I waited and waited, I noticed one positive sign right away: Reggie Langhorne was also at the signing, sitting right next to Bernie, no less. I knew Reggie knew me, as we had a great connection in the interview I did with him. In fact, after the Langhorne interview I went to the car dealership "Pat O'Brien Chevrolet" that he works for by my house, met with him again and he signed a photo for me. Reggie was just a great human being in every which way. I also noticed several people in line, with raggedy old Bernie Kosar Jerseys, ones that had to be at least 25 years old. His fans were so loyal and loved him so much, clearly he would be eager to give back to them, right?

As I approached Kosar, my palms were sweaty, my heart raced just a bit faster and I knew it was now or never to convince the local legend that even though he had fallen on hard times, his story was still vital and I was planning on telling it gloriously; I just needed his input to put it over the top and help me realize a dream of getting published by Triumph. As I hoped, Reggie spotted me right away and quickly nudged Kosar to tell him, "Hey, this guy is legit, you should speak with him about his book he is working on." Sadly, the pleas of Reggie would fall on deaf ears as Kosar had no interest in hearing anything from me other than checking my wristband to see if I paid the $25 to stand in line.

I pleaded with Bernie to listen to my story, or read the letter I wrote him, or by God even let me hang around the store until the signing was over so I could speak with him privately. He was not having it. As I walked away defeated, it dawned on me: he wanted money. So I turned back around and walked back into the store. The two hefty fellows running the signing instantly would try to play tough guy with me and let me know in no certain terms that I had my three seconds with the QB and it was now my time to leave. I yelled over to Bernie, "So, how much is it going to cost? " I had no intention on paying him, but curiosity got the best of me so I threw out a token number just to see what kind of reply I would get. "How about $2,000?" He laughed before replying, "It's going to cost you a hell of a lot more than that, kid."

For the first time in my five plus years of being a sports writer, I drove home defeated. Making the drive home even longer was that I bit into a peanut M&M and cracked my tooth wide open exposing a nerve. Despite the searing pain in my mouth at the moment, no pain was worse than seeing my chances at Triumph fly out the window. For the heck of it, I called 855-303-5450, the booking agency for booking an appearance by Bernie Kosar. The website is sportsspeakers360.com and sure enough right on the front of the Bernie Kosar page it tells you flat out that his fee is anywhere between $5,000 - $10,000. I asked the man on the other end of the phone if Kosar would possibly do it for less, and his response was cold and straight to the point: "No." He even went as far as to point out that for a book, he would probably charge more than the standard $10,000. I hung up the phone in disgust - Triumph was gone.

Now, don't me get wrong, I honestly don't blame Kosar. So many people have made money off of his name over the years, and so many people - Art Modell and others - have gotten rich off of his hard work and sacrifice of his body. It is a known fact that Kosar suffers badly from post concussion syndrome. It is only natural that the man would want to start cashing in himself and make some of his own fortunes back. I can only imagine how many get rich quick schemes people throw at him constantly. With that being said: old number 19, no hard feelings, I get it.

I tell this story because it is more than vital for one of the key reasons I chose to switch genres and write *Live to Inspire*. As I drove home that day I knew my life was destined for a change and that I needed to stop putting so much importance on sports. It was a cold, but needed wake up call. My mom had been begging me for years to write her story, a miraculous one of overcoming life crippling epilepsy to live a full and exceptional life. I had always promised her I'd write her story, but had let myself get consumed with sports writing over the years.

The Kosar mishap was sign one, and it wouldn't be too much longer until sign two came along. I was in full promotion mode, doing the radio and TV circuit for my latest book, *The Redemption of the King*. It was a book telling the story of the career of LeBron James, with the climax being his return to Cleveland in the summer of 2014. Sales and promotions were going fairly well when I appeared on my favorite morning show, "The Magic 105.7 FM Morning Show". It is one of the biggest ones on the dial and always a pleasure. It was during that interview that an idea struck me: this wasn't even a sports program and yet they continued to have me on. Wouldn't it be cool if I could talk about something on their show that may actually change lives and not just sports? With that large of an audience listening I felt that was a sign, that one day I needed to return to their show and talk about a message that could impact lives and give people hope instead of just balls and strikes.

As the Browns manuscript sat in author purgatory and several publishers prepared possible contracts for it, none of which were Triumph, I couldn't get too excited because the Kosar thing weighed heavily on my mind.

With the Kosar incident still ringing in my head and an uncertain feeling if a future in sports writing would continue to be my thing, I did what anyone should do when they are confused and in need of faith and answers: I went to church! I knew that if I was truthful to myself, didn't hide anything and just put it in God's hands, the answer would come.

As I sat in the pew praying, still disgruntled over Kosar, I got a third and final sign that confirmed the genre switch was coming from a higher power. There were these little pieces of white paper in each pew. They were empty ballots for Parish Council. Parish Council is a group of people elected by church members to meet once a month and help make important decisions that have to do with the direction of the church. At that moment something came over me. I don't why, and I don't know how, but this feeling of reaching out to God overcame me, so I didn't fight it. I reached over and put my name on one of the sheets of paper. I actually nominated myself to run for council. I never believed for a second I would actually get voted onto the council; after all, the church is huge and the vote would only be for 3 new members. As it turned out, several others were nominated as well, so the chances of me making the council were slim. I decided to run anyway and see what happened.

Eight days later, I woke up and couldn't breathe. Every breath I took hurt and hurt badly. My mom was there because she watches my daughter Maggie on Mondays while my wife Emily and I are at work all day. I stumbled to the living room in intense pain and white as a ghost. My mom instantly knew something was wrong and begged me to go to the emergency room. I refused to go, instead boldly and incorrectly making the asinine choice to go to work.

The biggest reason for the pain was because I had stayed up all weekend writing blogs and articles for my side job as an MMA correspondent for a website and then doing yard work for long hours in my yard. It was a weekend that saw too many Red Bulls and not enough sleep. I had no one to blame but myself for the self inflicted stupid torment done to my body.

The long hours combined with lack of sleep and stress over finding a good publisher for the Browns book became too much to handle, and hours later I found myself lying in a bed at Fairview Hospital being checked for a heart attack. The initial EKG revealed exactly that, as it looked as though my heart had gone on a roller coaster ride. Further tests would reveal (thankfully) that I didn't have a heart attack, but rather had torn several muscles in my chest, causing my breathing to be off and painful.

The next day my dad and wife, Emily, came to pick me up from the hospital and bring me home. The doctor told me to rest and not do anything for months. With Emily's and my parents' urging, I chose to listen to him; well, for at least a little while. He gave me these incredible pain killers which would knock me on my butt and allow me to breathe pain free, also allowing me to get some sleep. It was later that week during one of the long slumbers that my mom, who was visiting and checking in on me, came into my room with an envelope. It was from the church. I opened it fully expecting it to be a consolation letter telling me I didn't make parish council. To my complete and utter surprise, I made it. I was one of the top vote getters from my church. Sign three was received loud and clear: it was time for a change and time to give back to those with stories needing to be told, far more than any that a former quarterback could tell. Thus, a new book was born.

With the letter from the church I knew that the time for change was now and God was letting me know that the stories I needed to tell where right in front of me. Sure, I could and would still write about sports stars

- namely Vonda Ward - but not only would I tell her story on the mat, but also her more inspiring story in the fight of life where points don't matter, but heart does!

Stories of inspiration and overcoming incredible odds were the ones that mattered and needed to be told. Heroes are all around us, and I'm not referring to the millionaires on the gridiron or hardwood floors. I'm referring to the school teachers, the firemen and police men, the soldiers both male and female and anyone who puts their life on the line to secure the safety of others. I'm referring to the cancer survivors, people who have overcome epilepsy and those who battle and win against addiction every day. Their stories needed to be told!

These stories will give you reasons to believe, reasons to think that overcoming the impossible is possible and most importantly, these stories will let you know that no matter what hand of cards life may deal you, there is a never a reason large enough that you can't live every single day to inspire!

(authors note: Six months after the Kosar incident, I would receive a phone call from Bill Belichick, one of the greatest coaches in the history of pro sports. Not only did he not charge me for the phone call, but the man gave me 30 plus minutes of his time and thanked me for the chance to speak with me. I thanked him as well. This, friends, is why you never give up! God didn't want Kosar in the book, he wanted Bill and, I'm happy to say, I was signed to a publishing contract shortly after for it.)

Chapter One

PRAYERS FOR NOAH

"Life itself is the most wonderful fairy tale."

– Hans Christen Andersen

Noah Venesile came from a great home life, born to parents Chris and Amy Venesile on September 13, 2003. There was never a shortage of love in the Venesile home. Noah had several siblings to look up to as well, older sisters Paige and Sidney along with his oldest sibling, brother Nathan. They were always there to look after little brother Noah.

They were a musical family, as his father Chris was a music and choir teacher in the North Olmsted school system for 25 years from 1987 - 2012. Chris had graduated from The Ohio State University in 1982 with a Bachelor of Music education. Amy was well educated and very sharp herself, as she currently has a successful law career. They are two wonderful people, and the perfect parents to raise a large family.

Older sister Paige was excited to hear the news of a baby brother, as it was quite unexpected. She describes her emotions of hearing she was going to have a younger brother: ***"I was 8 when Noah was born, so I wasn't fully able to understand what it meant to have a baby brother, but I really loved having a baby around. Noah was a very cute baby, and he gave us something to be excited about. My parents sat my brother, sister, and me down on my brother's bed and told us. I don't remember perfectly, but I think we all told my mom we thought she was joking. When we realized she was serious, we were so excited. Looking back, I remember one night when my aunt came over and my mom said, "Go away!" and whispered something in my aunt's ear and she started screaming and cheering. Overall it was a great time for our family."***

The age difference between Sydney and Noah was seven years. A bit of a stretch between a third and fourth child, but God had his plan, and it was to bless the Venesile family with another child. Sydney was old enough to realize what it meant to be a big sister, and was quite excited to no longer be the youngest one of the bunch anymore. She reflects back on it now: ***"I was really excited to no longer be the youngest and I always loved kids, too. I then realized there was one drawback: his due date was close to my birthday and he ended up being born the day before my birthday. So as a seven year old little girl, I was a little jealous because they canceled my birthday party. So it is kind of funny now to look back at it. I love him to death, so it is okay to share a birthday with him now, but at seven I was bummed."***

Noah was very athletic, competitive and enjoyed playing team sports, but he hated to lose. He always pushed his teammates to be better with his hustle and aggressiveness. He played everything from baseball to basketball, and always gave things his best effort. He was also great inside of the classroom and had his father's ability for music, as he was a champion at piano playing and also sang in the choir. Noah had a zest for life and personality to go far in anything he did.

One of his heroes was Beatles legend George Harrison. So struck with the British icon was Noah that he soon developed an uncanny knack for impersonating the legend. He would put on his English accent and pretend to be him, even asking people to address him as such.

Older sister Paige recalls teaching him how to read and some of the close moments they shared: ***" I have more memories of Noah that I could ever think of on the spot. There is one thing that is very special to me. Both Noah and I love to read. I think that is something we share, because my other brother and sister aren't huge readers. When Noah was 4 (I think) and I was 12, I was the first person to teach him to read. I confirmed this with my mom because I wasn't sure if I remembered correctly. She said, 'Yep, you taught him how to sound out every letter.' Nathan, Sydney and I have a different relationship with Noah than we do with each other because of the age difference, but this is something that helped us to build a connection."***

He had an innocence about him along with a beautiful personality, with unlimited potential that could be spotted by anyone only minutes after meeting the young man. At the age of nine, it was already crystal clear that he had a bright future ahead of him if he could stay on the right track, which his family history proved he could and would.

Sydney explains a bit more about their own playful relationship and some very happy memories they shared that only strengthened their bond: ***"I remember coming home from high school, and he would be waiting for me in the kitchen and we would just turn on music and jam out together dancing and having fun. I was the closest to him in age and it really helped us have a playful relationship. We were rough with one another, too. He was tough and would put up good fight even when he was very little. He was a tough little boy. We would wrestle and tackle each other, but also sing together."***

It was November 6, 2012, Election Day all around Northeast Ohio. With issues and candidates on everyone's mind, ironically it would end up being someone too young to vote who would make the biggest impact of the day.

The polls were open and with local schools serving as voting sites, many kids were thrilled to enjoy a day off school from Westview Elementary School; one of which was 9-year-old Noah Venesile, who didn't waste the chance to play outside on such a beautiful day. It was while he was outside playing that a near tragedy occurred. In just a matter of seconds, this bright 9-year-old innocent little boy almost had all of it taken away from him. While playing in the front yard with neighborhood kids, Noah was focused on chasing a ball and didn't notice an approaching car. He darted into the street and was struck by the vehicle.

His older sister Paige was on the scene immediately, as she details here: ***"My sister Sydney and I were driving out of our neighborhood on our way to go shopping (it was election day and we had the day off school). When we turned left in the small intersection of our neighborhood, I saw one of our neighbors crouched on the ground in front of the curb, her back to us. There was another car parked in the street, and a woman standing next to it. Behind my crouched neighbor I saw a child lying on the ground, so I stopped. When I realized it was Noah and he was barely conscious, I threw the car in park in the middle of the intersection and got out and ran over to him.***

Things are kind of blurry from here. I remember I could barely get close enough to see him before I started screaming. My neighbor told us to call my mom, and I don't remember if it was Sydney or me who called. You could see our house from where we were standing and seconds later my mom sprinted out of the house towards us. I remember my best friend running outside because she could hear us across the street. The rest was waiting for the ambulance, which felt like an hour (it was probably less than 10 minutes). I think I'll always remember this as the worst day of my life. You never know what it will feel like to experience a trauma like this until it happens. Unfortunately, I found out when I was 17."

Sydney also looks back on that dark day: ***"We had just pulled out and we saw this crowd of people surrounding someone. I was scared it was Noah and then saw his shoe laying there and knew it was him. His eyes were shut and his face was pretty bad; it was a hectic state. My first instinct was to keep him moving and I kept talking to him, telling him I loved him over and over and begging him to wiggle his fingers. Some of it is a total blur. I tried to call my dad but I couldn't stop hysterically crying and screaming. My mom was screaming bloody murder, and when the ambulance came my mom went on the life flight and the neighbor took us. It was horrible."***

Chris had just started his new job at Kent State teaching music education when he received the phone call no parent wants to get. Chris looks back on that horrible moment: ***"I was in my office at Kent State on November 6, 2012. I was in my first year as Assistant professor of music education. I had texted back and forth with Noah, who had an iPod. It was a beautifully mild Election Day, with a day off from school for him and his sisters, who were at Avon Lake HS. I told him it was a beautiful day and to 'be a kid and get outside and run around!' I used to tell him that on nice days all the time. He responded to that with 'Har, har, har.' That was the last time he would be able to communicate with me for about 10 weeks.***

Noah took my advice and eventually got together with neighborhood friends (nearly 10) to play kickball on a corner lot near our house. Apparently, by the kids' testimony, the ball was kicked into the street and Noah was nearest to it and ran instinctively for it. A car tried to avoid him, but struck him, popped him up in the air and he fell headfirst onto the pavement. I received a call around 12:30 from my daughter Sydney. When I answered, it sounded as though she were laughing or messing around. I said, "Sydney, I'm working, what's up?" Then the phone went dead. A minute later I got a call from the neighbor lady whose home the kids were playing at. She said, 'Chris, there's been an accident, and Noah was hit by a car. He's not conscious and it looks bad; it looks like his jaw.'

Chris Venesile goes on to explain the thoughts running through his mind at the time of the call:*" My first thought was oh God, please don't let it be his head. Please let it be a broken bone, just not his head. After receiving the call, I was in a state of shock and stumbled down the hall to my colleague's office, where he tried to calm me down. I then called my wife who was in shock also, and she accompanied him on the helicopter flight to Metro Health Medical Center.*

I remember grabbing my things and getting in my car to drive to the hospital. I don't know why, but I was driving extra slow. When I arrived and the helicopter arrived, they placed my wife and I in the trauma room. There must have been a dozen people in that room waiting."

Avon Lake Paramedics reached him within 4 minutes and they secured him, administered medication to mitigate the damage being done to his brain, and the Metro Hospital Life Flight was dispatched to the ALPD to meet the paramedics. Noah was found with potentially serious life threatening injuries; combative with a high pitched shrill-like cry indicating a traumatic brain injury, and it was clear he needed transport to a trauma center. Acute Care Flight Nurse Practitioner Andrea Adoni and Flight Nurse Specialist John Singleton recognized the need for a rapid sequence intubation in order to protect his airway during transport. This was accomplished by the Life Flight medical crew, and together with the Avon Lake medics, Noah was prepped for his flight to Metro Health Medical Center.

Noah's mother Amy received a call that day that no mother would ever want to receive. She walks us threw her memories of the horrible day: ***"As Chris mentioned it was Election Day, November 6, 2012, and Noah was home since students had the day off school. It was a day I was working from home. Noah had been in and out of the house with his buddy all morning, and they went outside to play kickball or soccer at the neighbor's. Around noon I got a frantic call on my cell*** *phone from my neighbor. I immediately knew something was very wrong.*

My daughters had just left the house to go shopping and pulled down the street to see commotion. When they stopped the car they realized that their little brother was lying in the street. I ran out of the house with bare feet and could hear my daughters screaming - the kind that sounds more animal than human. I braced myself for what I would see. Noah was in the street on his stomach near the curb. He had lost a shoe and I could see blood coming from his nose. He wasn't moving at first, but after a few minutes he seemed to be struggling to try to get up. At least I knew he was alive.

My daughter Sydney called Chris, but her words were intelligible through her tears and panic, and my neighbor had to take over and deliver the awful news. It was an eternity in my mind before EMS arrived, but I logically knew it was only minutes; we live so close to the fire station. In some ways every detail was crystal clear, but it was like watching the scene from outside of my body.

I knew that Metro Life Flight was coming to transport Noah, but at that time he was still in the ambulance and I couldn't see him. One of the Avon Lake firefighters continued to check in with us to report what the paramedics were doing to stabilize him. A sick feeling in my gut was telling me that they were having a difficult time doing so. I'm not sure how long we waited at the fire station--even after Life Flight arrived we waited longer. They were probably still trying to stabilize him.

The passage of time was skewed I'm sure, but while we waited I asked my daughter to text my son Nate (who was away at college in Cincinnati) to call me immediately. He was in a class, but we told him to walk out of class and call. When I talked to him he just kept saying to me (not asking) "He's going to be ok. He's going to be ok. Right Mom?" I didn't have an answer for him, and he was alone and away from home and family. It ripped my heart out."

For a mother to see her child in this vegetable-like state and a bloody mess, it is a real life horror movie come to life. She continues to describe the nightmare: "*I don't think it happens too often, but I flew with Noah in the Life Flight helicopter. I had no recollection of the flight itself. I knew I was in a helicopter, but I think I was pretty deep in shock at this point. When we landed on the roof at Metro, the flight nurse asked me my son's name. "Noah. Venesile". He asked if his dad was Chris Venesile. That's when I realized why he looked familiar. I had met him through Chris at a number of choir concerts that Chris conducted. John Singleton is an outstanding medical professional who does his job with pride and efficiency--but I saw the pain on his face when he realized it was our son. Thank you, John, for the compassion you showed to us throughout our stay at Metro and beyond.*"

Amy continues the horrifying tale of the day that would forever change her life: ***"That's when the events of the day caught up to me and my legs gave out. I sat down for a bit and gathered myself. They took us to a waiting area. I think Chris's parents were waiting with us. I'm sure Chris called them on his way to Metro and they arrived pretty quickly, but details remain fuzzy for this period of time. We made calls, sent texts. I talked to my mom who lives in North Carolina. Having her so far away was painful for both of us. I have no idea what series of events was happening outside of the hospital, but after talking to the doctors and being told that Noah had suffered a brain injury, we found many of our friends waiting for us and waiting for news. We didn't have a prognosis for Noah. The doctors couldn't predict what would happen. We only knew that Noah's situation was critical. "***

Upon the arrival at the hospital, things looked bleak, but a familiar voice to the Venesile family signaled that perhaps a miracle was possible. Chris explains: ***"There was a trauma team at the hospital and the medical team was careful to stabilize him. They were ready and waiting for him with the Life Flight team. As they came down the***

hall (we were in the trauma room off to the side), I heard a familiar voice. It was the Chief Life Flight nurse, John Singleton. He had been a parent of a student at North Olmsted High School that I had taught choir at for four years. It was at that moment I remembered he was a nurse. After barking out the vital signs to the trauma team, he came over to us and offered his encouragement. He inquired about Noah each day when he arrived at work. He was our hero."

When there is brain trauma, there are certain biological processes that have to happen due to oxidation in the brain along with a breakdown of sorts after the trauma. Within an hour, if there aren't medical steps and treatments administered that they can give the patient, then the chance for saving the brain is almost impossible. The paramedics need to be there almost instantly to save a patient with brain trauma. By the paramedics getting there so quickly, it not only saved his brain, but also his life.

Noah was evaluated by the trauma team and, after a CT examination, his head was found to have a diffuse axonal injury, multiple facial fractures and a small epidural hematoma, in addition to some minor orthopedic injuries. He was admitted to the Pediatric Intensive Care Unit where he later had an intracranial pressure bolt placed due to elevated intracranial pressure.

Chris and Amy would later find out from the Hospital Chaplain, who was a high school student of Chris's dad in the 1960's, that Noah was not expected to survive the night. The next day, the chief intensive care neurologist said that Noah had sustained a severe head injury - a Traumatic Brain Injury. He showed them images of "white mass shearing" throughout his brain. That damage indicated that he may or may not regain consciousness and could very possibly remain permanently disabled or recover only partially. The Doctor said, ***"we hope for the best that Noah can be."***

The doctors couldn't give the Venesile family much hope or any false promises; things looked bad. They kept him in a coma as they tried to stabilize the brain, as they had no idea when he would emerge from the coma. Noah had an intracranial monitor that went through the skull and into the brain to check for brain swelling. In some cases, the brain needs room to swell, otherwise the pressure can become a big problem.

Everyone was in shock, as the Venesile family knew of the critical situation Noah was in. Immediately everything in their lives changed as they clung to hope for the young boy to make it. Chris discusses the adjustments that occurred: ***"We slept at the hospital for the first week. They gave us a place to greet family members and sleep and shower. Eventually I went back to work. Amy, who was working from home at the time, began staying at the hospital."***

The out pouring of emotion and support from friends and family was incredible, as Amy goes on to explain: ***"Metro has a wonderful waiting area near the PICU where friends and family could visit with us, hang out and be together. We pretty much took it over for at least two weeks--my apologies to other families who had children in the PICU at the time Noah was there. I'm sure at times the amazing PICU nurses felt overwhelmed by the sheer number of visitors that Noah had. But it sustained us through those most difficult days. We cherish all of you!"***

The support for Noah was felt not only city wide, but also nationwide. A Facebook page entitled "Prayers for Noah" was created within hours of the accident. In one of her earliest posts, Amy Venesile shared these emotional and heart wrenching words about her son's condition: ***" I never thought I would find myself in a position to be writing a post like this. I would give anything not to. What I can say is that despite how counterintuitive this may seem, I feel that for the first time in my life, I am truly experiencing God's Grace. The outpouring of concern for Noah and our family is astounding. We are wrapped in love, lifted by His spirit and honored to be included in your prayers. I know many of you are anxious for an update on his status, and I*** *wish we had more to share on his prognosis, but we are in the midst of a waiting game.*

Noah sustained a severe closed-head injury. He is being medically sedated, is on a ventilator to support his breathing while he is under sedation, and has a cranial pressure monitor in his skull (those words were so hard to type). He also sustained a fracture to his right ankle (which is currently splinted) and an orbital fracture around his left eye (thankfully the swelling has gone down significantly). Thankfully it doesn't appear he has any internal injuries to his core.

The most important focus right now is to keep his internal cranial pressure below 20, and right now he is at 9. Because of the type of brain injury Noah sustained, he could experience swelling in the next several days even though there is no swelling now. We hope for the best. He is doing exactly what the doctors want him to be doing for the present time.

I want more than anything for Noah to wake up and be exactly the same Noah he was before the accident, but this will be a long haul. He has youth on his side with respect to the brain being able to heal itself. So pray...continue to pray that God will let us have our Noah back with us, but we will take him however we can get him.

I'm going to lay down now in my little boy's hospital room and just watch him until I can fall asleep. Thank you everyone so very much.

With love and appreciation for all that God has given,

Amy

Noah was in a medically-induced coma for about 7 or 8 days. He was incubated and connected to a variety of life support machines including a feeding tube inserted into his stomach so he could still get nutrition. They tried unsuccessfully to bring him out of the coma one day and resumed a couple of days later, where they were successful. He remained in a stage called neurostorming, a time where the brain tries to reboot.

Neurological storming is a state that many patients experience after the heavy sedatives and painkillers leave the system. The sympathetic nerves and adrenal glands create a stress response after being stimulated by the hypothalamus.

Support from the community was instant as "Lights on for Noah" on November 10 occurred when Avon Lake residents were asked to turn on their porch lights that night as a sign of support for Noah.

It was difficult for his parents to watch as he was in great distress, eyes closed and not able to communicate. This is a horrible time for the patient as Noah was flailing and crying and didn't know what was going on. Despite being out of the medically induced coma, he still couldn't communicate and was in a natural comatose state. He had a cast on one of his legs that broke from the thrashing. In one instance he was thrashing so badly that the cast broke and came up and hit him the face, giving him a bloody and fat lip. The Venesile family urged the medical staff to give him medicine to lessen the thrashing and pain.

With his son comatose and fighting to stay alive, Chris instantly starting praying, but also started re-searching brain injuries. ***"I started researching head trauma injuries right away. Studying for my Doctorates Degree in Music Education really helped my ability to learn how to properly research a topic. What that means is that the scientific method, which is borrowed in natural sciences, is used in the social sciences. I did a lot of research on traumatic brain injuries. I wanted to find out how it was going to affect him 5 years from now, 10 years from now and thirty years from now. What did we know from past experiences from patients who had the same types of injuries? I wanted to find out!"***

Paige was devastated with what was going on with her younger brother, and had to look for various ways to cope with the daily pain. ***" I definitely realized how serious Noah's condition was. I think the doctors did a great job of making us aware that his future was***

uncertain. Traumatic brain injuries are almost always different. We were in constant communication with our parents, but we were at the hospital as much as possible so we kept ourselves informed. Early on, we kept busy by surrounding ourselves with other people and keeping busy. The first night after we went home, about 10 of our friends came over just to keep us company. Making sure I saw Noah every day was the main way I coped. I just needed to make sure I knew what his status was."

During the incredible heartache the family was suffering, there were some moments of hope and certain signs of life in Noah that kept the Venesile family clinging to hope. One of which was night 11, when one of the nurses asked Noah to give her a thumbs up and he did. There had been absolutely no communication at this point and no movement besides the thrashing. There was another instance of a nurse bathing him, and while she was washing his mouth, he started to pull away. The nurse commented how he didn't like that. Chris and Amy asked how she knew, and she said she just did and could tell. She gave them faith and pointed out that it was a good thing that Noah knew the nurse was there and doing something to him. She assured the Venesiles by saying, ***"Trust me, it looks bad now, but these kids - it happens. He will be better and running around like it never happened a year from now."*** At the moment, Noah wasn't even moving on his own, so the news provided hope.

Chris talks about the ray of hope given by the small movements from his son: ***"I could tell it was something special. I remember when he moved his little arm and raised his thumb. It was an emotional moment that left me in shock and happiness."***

On November 21, just 15 days after the accident, Noah was moved out of the PICU to the pediatric section. After almost three excruciating days of thrashing and agitation doctors finally administered a cocktail of sedatives that allowed him to get some rest.

On the morning of Nov 21, 2012, he had surgery to get a G-tube (feeding tube) and his leg was also casted while he was under. After the surgery, he was fairly restful and had a few wakeful times when he sat on his dad's lap and cuddled in bed. The plan was to manage the "storming" episodes as well as possible and hopefully transfer him to the rehab center ASAP.

On November 28, Chris posted the below message as he was lying next to Noah in the hospital bed. It was on the Facebook page "Prayers for Noah". Chris's words in this post sum up the pain and doubt he was feeling at this time as his son was battling for life: ***" It's midnight at the MetroHealth Medical Center. Noah is asleep and Amy is getting a rare night to sleep at home. It's been three weeks since the accident and in some ways feels like it's been three years. Other times, it feels like three minutes. Noah is going to be transferred to the Cleveland Clinic Children's Rehab facility in the next few days. He passed the swallow study today, meaning that he can swallow liquid or soft food well enough that he can protect his own airway to a degree.***

This all sounds positive, doesn't it? I've been getting congratulated a lot for all of these milestones he is passing. And I have been sharing these updates with a positive and optimistic zeal! I get that most (90%) victims don't survive or awaken, many are in longer comas, and still others have other serious injuries. So, of course I am thankful that he is somewhat conscious, breathing on his own, and occasionally is responsive (a smile most recently). But, I can't lie: I'm privately very scared about what lies ahead for Noah. I know I should be pumped up for the rehab, since I've heard that it is the best and that they work near-miracles. I've been told over and over how "strong" we have been, or "how well" we are handling it all. To be honest, I have been able to compartmentalize when I've left the hospital to go home or to work, but it's wearing off and it is now on my mind all the time--the bargaining, the weighing of the odds, the what ifs....

I believe that God has His plan. I'm just not convinced WHAT that plan is. A friend told me that I should not over-engage in fearful thoughts, as God doesn't deal in fear - His plan is His plan. I like that idea, but am not sure it makes me feel any better. Faith, when put to this kind of test, is a real test! And tough! All I know is that I look into those eyes that, in a week, won't even look like he's ever been in a near fatal pedestrian/car accident, and will wonder how much of life he will reclaim. I think maybe it is about accepting the outcome. The daily outcome, weekly, monthly , and yearly. I've always been successful at breaking down big things into smaller, easier-to-accomplish things."

Through the power of constant prayer and incredible medical treatment, Noah kept hanging on and wouldn't let the horrible accident take his life. It was about three weeks before he was able to respond facially. He could not speak; he was unable to speak, eat, walk, or go to the bathroom for six weeks. He was moved to a step down unit at Metro after two weeks and stayed there for two weeks. He was then transferred by ambulance to the Cleveland Clinic Children's Rehabilitation Center in Shaker Heights. At the end of the first week at CCC Rehab, Noah started to show dramatic improvements in his progress. He began to speak slowly, and his motor skills were improving.

Once things began to slowly get better, he developed a wandering eye. He would eventually be able to open both eyes and stop thrashing around. There was one day in particular that stands alone as a breakthrough in his recovery: his sisters brought one of his dogs to the hospital, a mini golden doodle named Delia, to see him. The dog was so excited to Noah, that she instantly tried jumping in bed with him. Upon seeing this, his face lit up with emotion for the first time since the accident. It was one of those little miracles that started to happen.

Paige was lucky enough to be a part of this special moment with her father and brother. ***"I was there the first time Noah smiled. My dad***

and I brought one of our dogs, Delilah, to the hospital after getting it approved by the staff. We brought her on his bed and he smiled. It was the most heartwarming experience I've ever had. I cried immediately. Noah came out of his coma pretty slowly in the sense that it took him a while to be able to communicate. I can't remember the first time I heard his voice specifically, because he was making sounds before he was saying words. Just hearing him attempt to communicate gave me so much hope."

Chris remembers one moving story of when Noah still hadn't come completely out of it, but was beginning to show signs: ***"One day I just grabbed him and put him in my arms to sit with him in a chair. I held him real close, and his body just seemed to relax. It was as if his body was in this cocoon of safety while he was in my arms. He reacted to my body heat and went limp and relaxed. It was a moving moment and I will never forget; it was total pure love for my child."***

The Venesile family continued to cling to hope that Noah would return to normal one day, and along the way they continued to get little signs that it may just happen. There were monumental moments of celebration, such as when he could sit up without help. Another big miracle was when he could hold something on his own, or eat and swallow on his own.

The rehab center helped tremendously as it allowed Noah to have his own room, including one-on-one attention from doctors, psychologists, occupational therapists, physical therapists, teachers and every benefit you can think of. He was on the schedule of all of the therapists around the clock along with top notch nursing care.

Once again, the rehab did not come without struggles. There was one day in the search for finding Noah that the Venesile family brought in his iPad in the hopes of familiarity for him to help with his recovery of memory. Noah grabbed the iPad, but started crying afterwards because he couldn't get his brain to tell his fingers what to do to manipulate it.

He threw his head back out of frustration. There were several tender moments as well, such as his grandfather John coming into the room to hold him in his arms for a long period of time.

Sydney found her own special way to share moments with Noah, even in moments of darkness that lifted both of their spirits: ***"we always have had this playful relationship with one another where we pretend to fight and just buddy around. It was during a visit that we tested this a little. My mom took his hands and made fists for him to punch; he was still out of it, but also still there in a way. My mom asked him who he wanted to punch, then she said my name and he made a groan of approval and smiled. That was a great sign that he was able to remember our relationship."***

As all of this was going on, his big sister Paige was applying for colleges, many of which required essays along with the application. It was during this process that she wrote this beautiful essay along with her application to Ohio State University: ***"I can't say I have many standout memories from when I was eight years old, but there is one I will never forget. The day my parents told my brother, sister and me that we were going to have a new baby. On September 13, 2003, Noah was born. I was so overjoyed to be able to call this baby my own brother. Fast-forward nine years to the most life-changing day I could imagine. It was Tuesday November 6, 2012. It was Election Day, which means there was no school in our district. Without school, Noah decided to play with all of the neighborhood kids down the street. As I drove out of the neighborhood to run an errand, I saw commotion on the street. I got out of the car to find out Noah ran into the street for a ball and was hit by a car. He was unconscious. I heard the sirens of an ambulance, refusing to believe it was my brother it was coming for. After a long day, family and friends finally got to see Noah at the hospital. It was a heartbreaking sight, seeing my 60-pound brother sedated, attached to IVs and breathing tubes with a brain monitor protruding from his head. He had a broken eye socket, leg,***

and serious brain injuries, which are the reason for his sedation. If there is one person who does not deserve a fate like this, it's this little boy. The brilliant boy I taught to read at age three, who continues to have a passion for it. The boy who loves Spongebob Squarepants, video games, laughing, Cheez-Its, and playing pranks. The first week was the hardest. After about seven days, Noah was taken out of sedation, and his breathing tube was removed. Ten days after that, Noah smiled for the first time since the accident upon seeing a picture of our six-month-old Golden Doodle puppies, Dexter and Delilah. Today, Noah is unable to communicate verbally, as the only real form of communication has been crying. Although many of the signs seem negative, Noah is making baby steps in a positive direction. Yesterday marked the three-week point since his accident, and in a few days he will be moved to a rehabilitation center. I try to spend as much time as possible with my brother, whether it be talking, playing a game, or simply watching TV together, because he always inspires me and brings so much joy into my life. In these past three weeks I have frequently missed this quality time. However, even without the ability to communicate with Noah, he has inspired me more than ever before. I can see his desire to pull through this struggle with the strength he has always had, and I have no doubt that because of him I have, and will continue to, become stronger."

The initial assessments were not good, and things continued to look bleak, but Noah would not stop fighting and eventually would have a breakthrough. There was an educator working for Cleveland public schools, but also working for the hospital. He would come in everyday to work with kids at the facility. Before the accident, Noah was a straight-A student, reading at a fifth grade level in the third grade. He wasn't speaking clearly at this point, but he was communicating a little bit with his hands.

The hospital had a book they were using to keep track of his progress and at the end of every day they would have Noah sign his name. The first slew of days, he was barely able to scratch the paper with anything but light markings. Then one day, a few weeks in, a miracle would happen, as Noah was able to write his entire name on the note pad. He began to improve as his motor skills began to return.

The road to recovery would be a long one, but Noah had the fighting spirit to make it happen. He began rehab to relearn how to walk, getting the brain to recognize and relearn the process. After six weeks, he began to ride a three wheeler and walk a bit. The doctors and medical staff were doing everything they could to get his brain working again on many different levels.

Chris explains just how hard it was to watch his son struggle to do even the littlest of tasks: ***"It was hard to watch him struggle, but even harder than watching that was the constant worrying if he would ever return back to normal. It is one thing to watch someone struggle, but if it is temporary then you know the conclusion is forgone; with this we had no idea. We didn't know if he would ever get better. Watching him struggle was hard, but it was so much harder not to think about him having to be in this state for the rest of his life. As a parent in this type of ordeal, you do feel helpless."***

It was a difficult time, but Chris remembers how his family and faith came together in the face of adversity: ***"We closed ranks and faced Noah's recovery together. Our close friends and family helped us immeasurably during this time. It made me realize that the power of prayer is real, since his Facebook page was reaching tens of thousands of people who were praying for his recovery."***

He was granted a surprise six hour visit on Christmas Eve to his grandparents home, where his whole family had gathered. The visit was almost more for his family then him, as they so badly wanted to see him standing and being able to speak to them. It was an emotional night.

Sydney remembers the night her brother came home for a visit on Christmas Eve well: ***"That was amazing because it was a surprise to the rest of our family because they didn't know he was coming, so it***

was just so emotional and overwhelming with joy. It is such a special holiday and we are such a tight knit family that is was amazing to have him home."

The prayers worked and, on February 1, 2013, after 56 days in the hospital, Noah was allowed to go home for good as he was released into outpatient care. Noah did not suffer permanent memory loss. He does, however, have no memory of that day, a few weeks before and about six weeks after the accident.

During his recovery, the Venesile family was flooded with grief and heartache, but also large medical bills. While some of them were covered with insurance, most were not and the community, upon hearing of Noah's story, decided to help out the family. There were two fundraisers in his honor, one in Parma by the families at the Brew Garden. The other was held at Avon Oaks Country Club by friends in Avon Lake, emceed by Avon Lake resident and TV personality Ron Jantz.

Ron Jantz proved that he was more than just a local celebrity, but rather an incredible human being as well with his actions towards the Venesile family during the hard times they were suffering from.

Ron Jantz got his start in Cleveland Media in 1987 as he worked with WUAB Chanel 43 from 1987 to 1994. While there, he got the chance to work with one of his media heroes, Gib Shanley. Jantz explains that being on TV was not always his dream: ***"Honestly, I didn't really watch the news that much. I was too busy playing sports, on a ball field or with my friends in the yard. When I was in my middle teens though (14-18), I listened to the Browns on the radio and it was always Gib Shanley that I enjoyed listening to."***

Ron goes on to explain that even if his initial plans weren't for broadcast journalism, it was some words of wisdom and guidance that led him down that path: ***" I started at Lorain County Community College. It was one of the best decisions I made. I was encouraged by a professor at LCCC to get into broadcasting (I came to college***

thinking I wanted to be a writer – print journalism). He steered me toward television. I knew going into LCCC that I wanted to transfer after two years (associate degree) to Ohio University and try and get into the E.W. Scripps School of Journalism. I was able to do that, and I graduated from OU's Scripps School with a Bachelor's Degree in Journalism (with honors) in 1987."

With his infectious personality and warm demeanor, Jantz had no issues making the transition from WUAB 43 to WKYC Chanel 3 in 1994, where he stayed from 1994 - 2000. He would eventually take a job closer to home with Lorain County Community College as their digital Coordinator. The job at LCCC - as opposed to being on TV - gave him more time to be with his family. He has a wife Stacy and four children: Riley, Julia, Caroline and Maggie. He was a family man, and that is why the story of Noah resonated with him upon hearing of it for the first time. Ron goes on to explain how he first heard of the accident to young Noah: ***"My son Riley and one of Chris's daughters (Sydney) were in the same grade in high school. They both sang in the ALHS Chorale. Music would bring us to the same events. So, I knew of them. I heard of the accident from my wife, Stacy. She had heard about it from friends in the community. Avon Lake is a pretty small community. I think we are around 23,000 residents, and if you have children in the schools that number gets even smaller. So, when something happens to or with a family, the news travels pretty fast."***

As a parent of four children himself, Ron talks about how hard it was for him to hear the news of a child almost being killed: ***" How hard is it? It makes your body go numb when you hear the news. I think any parent would give you a similar answer. Why? Because you know the love that you have for your own children. You know how you try to protect them from danger. You know you can't always protect them, too. We see our children as innocent. We hurt when that is broken. Parents can relate, I think, to each other's challenges – even when they aren't the same."***

With the professionalism and character of Ron Jantz, he was a natural fit to emcee the event at Avon Oaks on March 9, 2013 for Noah and the Venesile family. Ron remembers: ***"A friend of mine (Pam Ohradzansky) called me on my cell one day. I was working out over my lunch break and stopped to grab my cell. It was winter, late January I think. She asked if I would consider emceeing a fundraiser she was helping organize for Noah and the Venesile Family. I said yes, immediately. Like I said, we are a tight knit community. People respond. People step up. It was the least I could do. It was my honor to be asked."***

It was a great night with plenty of action and support for Noah. Things could have went much differently, but the experience and poise of Ron Jantz kept things together, as he explains:***" It was happy. It was busy. I have emceed events at Avon Oaks before and the banquet room is not a great place to work the crowd as an emcee. It is long and skinny and you are in the middle of it – so there is no real front. You have people far away to your left and far away to your right. It is hard for those people to hear you because you are not projecting your voice in one direction – forward. When you look right, the people to the left can't hear or see you and vis-a-versa.***

It's a difficult room to work and I knew that going in – so I prepared everybody for it in my opening comments on how we were going to attack the live auction. In that setting, you REALLY need the cooperation of everyone in the room. If anyone is talking or holding their own conversations while you are trying to work the room, then it becomes challenging for others to hear.

That said, the people in attendance responded well! We had their full attention and the live auction went well. Noah was there. His parents and siblings. The band Train donated a signed guitar. One of the members of Train was a student of Chris's at North Olmsted High School. That was cool.

Again, the connection to family and community that we all have is why everyone was there. On that night, it wasn't our child or our

family, but it could have been. You stand for each other. That's what it really comes down to. I believe every one of us in life has a gift to give. It could be anything. Once you identify what your gift is, you should share it every chance you can. Every person that night had a gift to give to Noah and his family. Every person. Some, it was financial. Others, their dedicated time. Some, their prayers. Others, support through meals or car rides for the other kids or just checking in. It's a lot like a team and community. If we all do our part, if we all consider others, if we all look past ourselves, it can work beautifully."

Amy gives thanks to those responsible for helping raise funds for Noah and his treatment: ***"The fundraisers were wonderful and the credit goes to our families, friends, and community. Humility abounds after such an extraordinary show of support and love towards Noah and us. No words could ever express our gratitude."***

Noah was able to attend them both for very a brief time length, and was able to speak briefly to the enormous crowd of people there to support him. People were incredibly generous and donated everything they could to help raise money. One couple even donated a week at their Florida condo. Both fundraisers were beautifully done, and they raised over $50,000.

The story of Noah was inspiring to all of those who heard it, and several media outlets chose to cover it. Every local and Cleveland news organization did stories on his recovery, including Fox 8, WKYC, the Cleveland Plain Dealer, Avon Lake Press and several other outlets.

Noah was saved by the quick action taken in the ***"Golden Hour"*** after injury. The human brain is truly amazing. He also benefited from being at an age of development that worked in his favor. We must never give up hope that kids can overcome what seems like an injury that will be debilitating. He was lucky in many ways, but the power of prayer surely can account for the fact that, even though his personality changed a bit (he is more laid back, philosophical now; less coordination, but more artsy), he has restored cognitive function, requires no special care by any physician, no accommodations at school, and his grades are excellent.

On February 9, 2013, three plus months after the accident, Noah went to visit the Avon Lake first responders who responded to the call the day of the accident. ***"You guys are so special,"*** Noah told Avon Lake Fire Department and Metro Life Flight members as he gave each one a hug. The Metro Life Flight helicopter landed at the fire house just for him. Shortly after, dressed in a pilot's helmet and jacket, Noah gave a huge smile and a wave from the chopper's cockpit.

The more that people learned of his tale, the more it inspired those who heard it. The 11 Foundation chose Noah as one of the recipients of the Nick Ventura Determination Award a short while after. The 11 Foundation was formed to assist families struggling through the recovery of a loved one who has suffered a traumatic brain injury.

As the word continued to spread of his heroic recovery, several media outlets contacted the Venesile Family for the story, including Parade Magazine which decided to produce a Holiday Video on Noah's Story.

Even though his recovery was nothing short of a miracle, there were still plenty of painful times and discouraging setbacks that reared their ugly heads six months following the accident during his first baseball practice, as his father Chris explains: ***" Noah was one of the better players on his coach-pitch team the prior year, hitting the ball solid and fielding and throwing above average for his age group. I was with silent horror when we began playing catch outside a few weeks prior to his first practice after the accident. It was like turning the clock back three years. He had great difficulty catching and making routine throws. Like his speech had been, everything was S-L-O-W. The arm following through was slow, so the ball was slow and bounced to me regularly.***

The first practice came and, because it rained, it was indoor. Our coaches, Jeff and Jaime, knew of Noah's injuries and we talked about

how we would deal with them. I wasn't sure about the other players, since Noah didn't know them personally, but I gathered that his case was well known to them.

It was a struggle, but we got through it. Once in the car, it was one of the first times since the accident that I knew that Noah was in full realization of the scope and long-term implications of his injuries. 'Dad, I can't believe how bad I stink now!' As I put a positive spin on it, I got a lump in my throat knowing how hard the game of baseball can be for lots of 9-year-old boys, let alone one who had a TBI, skull fractures, eye socket fractures, and a broken leg. Metaphorically, it represented the entire landscape of his recovery-- finally self-assessing the reach of his handicaps, whether temporary or not. And by using the word 'handicap,' I mean 'something that hampers or hinders' performance. 'I'm small and wimpy and I'm not good, can I quit?' For a moment, I wondered if it might be too soon."

This was also one of the first times that the reality of what he missed while he was away from school and in recovery fully sunk in. As Chris was tucking him in later that night after the first baseball practice, Noah sounded discouraged for the first time as he told this to his dad: ***"'I wish this dumb accident never happened'" finally came out of his mouth. "'We got our yearbooks today and I am missing from so much! Thanksgiving pictures, Christmas pictures....I LOVE all that stuff--and I missed it!'"***

Knowing that damage control was in need and his son in serious need of a confidence boost for the first time in his life, like any good father would, Chris sprung into action: ***"We talked about our human interaction with time and our inability to go back in time to 're-do' things in our lives. I mentioned that if we could go back in time, most of us would never see our futures. There were tears and a real acceptance of loss, but also a return to a focus on future goals.***

I tucked him in and said goodnight and went downstairs for a few minutes. When I returned upstairs to my room Noah opened the door and said, 'I just wanted to say thanks for talking to me.' In that statement I heard some resolution and 'coming to terms.' More importantly, I felt that in his desperation he also found a soft place to land for a while."

Outside of just sports, Noah still faced uphill battles in other facets of his life: ***"School had its ups and downs--math facts were a barometer of what's going right or wrong on a daily basis. Though Noah's progress had been steady, we at home see it less than those who see him only occasionally. His desire to return to "normal" has been realized: his best friends are still his best friends, they do sleepovers and play video games and engage in bathroom humor. His latest CT scan had shown a decrease in brain swelling--months after the accident! In the new scans, the neurologist says that it may look "normal" at some point. Normal, of course, is a relative term. We have a new normal, and in many ways it's a better normal. For me, the compass seems set on a clearer vision of the future. For the rest of our immediate and extended family, it seems that along with the new normal comes a decrease in sweating the "small stuff."***

Nine months following the accident, Dr. Khoushik, pediatric neuropsychologist, put Noah through two half-day tests to measure all dimensions of his cognitive functioning. The results of those tests were astounding.

Dr. Khoushik stated that even though Noah has some coordination issues and slower processing speed in some areas along with fatigue, the report states that "the results of this assessment suggest that he is doing remarkably well from a cognitive perspective. Importantly, over-estimated intellectual functioning is better than 91% of his peers.

When we asked if his injuries were not as severe as once thought, the Dr. said, ***"No, I would constantly review the brain scans following***

his admittance to the hospital and was in disbelief that he could be doing this well after such devastating injuries." While he didn't use the word "miracle," he did say he was "astounded" and "amazed." Drs., of course, don't use those terms very often, if at all. Dr. Khoushik also stated that he has so many cases that he could say that he has had many children with less severe injuries do much poorly afterward.

The woman who hit Noah filled out the police report and was never heard from again. As most people would have followed up with the family or stayed in touch with the hospital to see how he was doing, she chose not to. In a further show of class and maturation from Noah, he was never bitter about this, and instead thanked the woman from the Facebook page his mother created entitled "Prayers for Noah". The post came on the one year anniversary of his accident: ***"Hi! I'm Noah! I really appreciate everyone praying for me in the hospital and who helped support me when that rough accident happened. I'm doing great now because of you guys! I'm doing well in school, taking hip-hop dance lessons, and playing piano. And I want the driver of the car to know that it's alright, and we all make mistakes sometimes. So you don't have to be embarrassed. But if you're too shy to meet me, I totally understand. Now, I know how hard it would be if I didn't make it through that accident. But I made it thanks to your guy's wishes and prayers!***

Love,

Noah

Sister Paige reflects back on how far things have come, and how proud she is of her brother years later: "***Unfortunately, I am at school at Ohio State most of the year. When I do get breaks, I hang out with Noah when he's not off playing with friends. Noah and I never really play physically, we mostly like to hang out. We like to watch a lot of movies together. Since Noah's injury is fully healed, I don't treat him any different than I would if he had never been injured.***

I could not be more proud of my brother. He has been such an inspiration to me, along with countless others. He had to work so hard to get where he is today. As for those who helped my family, I could never say thank you enough. I couldn't begin to explain the amount of support we received from family, friends and members of our community that we didn't even know.

For anyone going through the same experience that I did, I would say to show him/her as much love as you can. I believe that Noah, even when he wasn't fully aware, knew that his family was there for him. Support your other family members, as well. They are hurting just as much, and a little support goes a long way."

Sister Sydney agrees with Paige in her pride of Noah as she also looks back on it three years later: ***"I'm so proud of Noah, and it is crazy to think back now, but everything does happen for a reason. I'm a firm believer of that, and Noah even says that he wouldn't change it because it made him who he is now. He is the one person I know who could have overcome all of this. His spirit and determination are so strong, and he overcame all of it. He is healthy and just a normal kid now, almost as if it never happened. He is so normal, happy and strong.***

I would tell anyone who ever has to go through something like this to pray and keep having faith because miracles do happen, and what happened with Noah is nothing short of a miracle. If he could do what he did, then I think anyone can do anything they put their mind to!"

Amy Venesile had this to say looking back on her son's accident, but also the help and prayers that led to his road to recovery: ***"It is cathartic for me to write out all the details of November 2012. I've told bits and pieces of what I remember to friends, but to have it all in one place and in order helps me come to terms with it. I will say that while I never questioned my faith - nor did I question why God would let this***

happen to our son - I have many times questioned why some families aren't as fortunate in the recovery of their loved ones. It's the thing that troubles me most of all. I pray for it to happen for them as it has for us. One of the reasons we have participated in fundraising campaigns for MetroHealth and Cleveland Clinic Children's Hospital (where Noah did his inpatient rehab and continues as an outpatient in therapy), is that we hope their programs help give other families the best possible care for the best possible outcome. Of course, Noah loves participating in those campaign's because he's an unapologetic ham.

The regret I carry throughout this journey is that we didn't have the where-with-all to keep track of every person who sent food, generous gifts, letters, wine (oh never mind--I remember who sent that). Seriously, we did our best to write it down or take a photo to remind us, but I know we missed people along the way and some did not get a proper "thank you". Please know that we appreciate everything that was done for our family. We needed every single uplifting comment and prayer that was offered to get us through this incredible journey, and we've read them all. May God be with all of you in your journey through life. May His peace be with you always. You have touched our lives, and we are forever grateful."

Perhaps Ron Jantz summed it up best when it comes to Noah, as he had these lasting words: ***" Every now and then in life, you meet someone who is magnetic. You meet a person that everyone is attracted to. Noah is that type of kid. He has a smile that will melt you. A little voice you want to capture in a box and save it forever and a stage presence he carries that you are simply just drawn to. He wouldn't know me from Adam if I walked up to him, but I know him. He's that type of kid."***

Chris explains how his son is today, over three years later: ***"He is what I call 'Noah version 2.0.' Large chunks of him are the same, but he has new dimensions to his personality. He is still like a little adult,***

but waxes philosophical and has a great sense of humor. His outlook hasn't changed at all since just after recovering. He says, 'I am not sorry the accident happened. It has helped make me who I am today, and I like who I am.'"

Chris has these words of advice for any parent who is forced to endure such a horrible ordeal: ***"I hope that people can derive some comfort knowing that miracles really do occur. His prognosis was not good by any team of doctors, yet he made huge strides due to his spirit and determination. He was surrounded by love from his family, friends, neighbors, and community. His school and teacher and principal were unbelievably supportive, and we were the beneficiaries of the good in people. You don't realize how good people can be - and certainly would not want to find out the way we did - but it is amazing and transforms you.***

One of my enduring memories of faith and humanness of that horrible day was the fact that my best friend since I was 13, Mickey Vittardi, stayed with me from that afternoon until the wee hours of the morning and provided comfort, strength, and support. Mickey's own father died that morning."

If we could all learn one thing from Noah Venesile, it would be that nothing can take your smile, your spirit and most importantly, your future! His body never gave up, his mind never gave up and his soul never stopped fighting. At nine years old, this little boy fought tougher battles then most people ten times his age see in a lifetime. Noah Venesile is a fighter, a champion and a symbol of how life should be lived, because you never know when that next ball may bounce in the street of life.

Chapter Two

SUPER BABY

"Fate whispers to the warrior, you cannot withstand the storm.

The Warrior whispers back, I am the storm!"

Life does not always turn out the way you plan and, more often than not, you don't get what you want. We all have our stories. Some of our stories can be a small struggle in our lives, while others force us to challenge all that we know. These rough circumstances can change the course of our lives. How someone chooses to respond to it is what really matters. Perhaps life is showing you where you need to grow and is leading you to the person you were meant to be.

Jennifer Urban Kunes was born in October of 1977 at Fairview Hospital and grew up in North Olmsted, Ohio. She has a younger brother named Rob who is only 11 months younger. Growing up, she enjoyed various activities with family and friends. Her favorite vacation with her family was going to Niagara Falls. She was very active in school, where she played several sports growing up and also did dance. When she got into middle school she focused on volleyball, basketball, and softball.

Despite her talent for sports, her greatest gift was that of being a natural at nurturing and teaching. This was made evident when she attended Cleveland State University and received her Bachelor of Science in Environmental Science. Instead of looking for a job at NASA or in a lab somewhere, she decided to give back to the community and help mold today's precious youth by becoming a high school science teacher in the suburbs of Cleveland.

With her career well under way and a lot of love to give in her heart, she met her husband Ralph through an on line dating site called Match.com. She signed up for the site on a whim, as it was her Christmas break from teaching and she was looking for something new to try with her time off. It was only a month trial membership, but it would end up changing her life.

Ralph was born in June of 1971 in Cleveland, Ohio and grew up in Brooklyn, where he attended Brooklyn High School. He was a three-sport athlete in high school, as well as he excelled in cross country, wrestling and track. He also enjoyed skiing in the winter and Cedar Point in the summer. He eventually attended Kent State and then went onto a career in real estate.

They began dating and soon fell in love. They liked to visit Put in Bay, an Island in Northeast Ohio near Sandusky. Ralph owned a house up there and they would make frequent visits. They talked about having a family one day, and hoped to have four kids. They also enjoyed going to watch pro boxing fights together. It didn't take Ralph long to realize Jennifer was the one for him and he proposed marriage eight months into their relationship. On December 8, 2007, Ralph proposed to Jennifer in Niagara Falls while sitting at a bar in a restaurant waiting for their reservations at Skylon Tower. A short while after, they got married on August 9, 2008 at Saint Ignatius of Antioch in Cleveland.

Jennifer and Ralph wanted to have kids. They both talked about it while dating and hoped to have four kids right away. They were anxious to become parents together and have a big family full of love and memories. God answered their plans and prayers, as they didn't have to wait long and Jennifer found out she was pregnant with their son Brock on October 8th 2008. Just 4 days before, she was celebrating her 31st birthday after playing competitive co-ed football all morning. Life was good!

At 31 years old and 38 years old respectively, the lives of Jennifer and Ralph would change forever nine months later on June 17, 2009, when their son Brock was born. What should have been a joyous occasion for the couple turned into a nightmare when things began to go wrong. Jennifer had been induced into labor the night before around 6pm, but things did not go smoothly.

The labor began to stretch on, and the next thing they knew it was 2am and she was stuck at 9 centimeters. The time for pushing would eventually begin as she finally reached 10 centimeters. The pushing did not go as planned, and she would end up pushing for 3 and a half hours. The doctors tried doing a vacuum twice, but it didn't work. The room was flooded with nurses and doctors but nothing seemed to work. It was a chaotic scene and the medical staff had to make a judgment call, as things were becoming very dangerous. They ordered an emergency caesarean section as Jennifer was crying and shaking uncontrollably from the massive blood loss she had just endured. The blood was everywhere; it appeared as if someone was murdered. Things would go from bad to almost tragic soon after.

Jennifer looks back on this hard time: ***" I remember thinking to myself I'd be okay if I died now. I had this incredible feeling of exhaustion that is quite unexplainable. I felt like I was done fighting, almost at peace. I just wanted my baby to be born. When they pulled Brock out, he didn't cry or make any noise, and it was very scary. We were afraid he wasn't breathing. The doctors rushed Brock over and began doing suctions to help him and get him breathing. Finally one***

of the doctors turned over to us and gave us the thumbs up. Within seconds of that, we heard Brock cry for the first time. They wrapped him and brought him over to me to see, but I wasn't able to hold him, they just took him away. That is the last thing I remember before waking up in the recovery room."

Brock was a large and healthy 9lbs. 15oz and 21.5 inches at Southwest Hospital in Middleburg Heights. He did have an infection because Jennifer's water was broke for almost 24 hours. He was born at 5:41 pm in the evening, but Jennifer would not get to hold him because of the medical issues she had to endure. Around 11pm that night Jennifer required a blood transfusion of 2 pints. By the time she was able to hold Brock briefly, he was already over 24 hours old. It was the first time she got to hold her son, but it was only for minutes before the nurses had to take him back to the NICU.

The joy of being parents was suddenly gone, as she was kept from her son for days until she was able to walk down to the ICU and see him again. Her feet were so full of fluids that they actually made squishing sounds as she walked. As she slowly walked down the hall, in intense pain both physically and emotionally, she was determined to see her son and hold him. A few days later they were able to reunite and go home as a family.

The early scare couldn't stop their extreme excitement to be parents, and they fit into the role naturally. Jennifer left her job as a full-time teacher to spend as much time with her baby boy as possible. ***"I was a stay-at-home mom with Brock. I would substitute once in a while if I needed some extra funds. We had planned to have 4 kids right away, but things did not work out that way. I went back to work full-time in August 2013."***

They enjoyed taking Brock to the park, the zoo and doing things outdoors with him. They took him to the islands quite a bit; boat rides with family and other such adventures. Like his parents, Brock took to sports naturally and began playing soccer and T-Ball at the age of three. They would take him to Kiddy Park and Cedar Point. It was important to them to keep active and make sure their son had great memories.

Just as expected, they loved being parents and decided to start trying to have their second child right away. This time, things weren't as easy as they were in conceiving Brock, and the challenges and setbacks were endless. Over the next four years, they faced every issue possibly, including a miscarriage. Jennifer explains some of the setbacks and extremely hard times: ***"We started to try to have another baby when Brock was 4 months old. We tried for 4 years and 1 month before we conceived Briana. I was diagnosed with Secondary Infertility. We tried several different methods of fertility treatments. We went through 3 failed rounds of Clomid, 2 failed rounds in Intrautrine Insemination (IUI) with Follistim injections, 1 failed "Fresh Transfer" of In Vitro Fertilization(IVF): 3 embryos transferred. 1 successful "Frozen Transfer" of IVF: 2 embryos transferred which resulted in twins.***

These were very dark days during those 4 years. I cried more times than I could possibly remember. I asked God all the time, 'Why me?!?!' The pain would come back, like clockwork every month. I had such an agonizing mixture of failure, heartbreak, frustration, and anger. I was terribly depressed seeing my friends have babies. Some had multiple babies in those four years we were trying to conceive. It was the first time in my life that I could not control what was happening to me. It was when I truly learned what struggle meant. Why was this so easy for everyone else but me? I was so thankful for Brock, though. He was such a good boy. I just so desperately wanted to give him the gift of a sibling. Someone he could play with, share stories and memories with; just someone who will be there for him when Ralph and I are no longer here. I knew he would be the best big brother! There definitely were times that I thought maybe I was only going to have one child."

Success would finally come, and in early January 2014, Jennifer and Ralph got the news they had longed prayed for: they were pregnant once again. They were both thrilled at receiving the news of the pregnancy. It was a surreal moment they thought they would never get to experience again.

Sadly, once again, the happy moments did come with some eventual horrible moments and terrible losses. They found out early on that they were having twins and were ecstatic at the thought. It was at an ultra sound in March, however, that they were once again given bad news. Jennifer remembers how hard it was to find out: ***"I had to go to a lot of Ultrasounds because I was at an advanced maternal age, '36.' I was at Fairview Hospital and it started off as a pretty typical ultrasound. The ultrasound technician was taking pictures and not really saying a whole lot. She sent me to the bathroom and asked me to pee, because she thought if I emptied my bladder, she would get some better pictures. I knew right then something was not right. I knew I did not have a full bladder. After returning from the bathroom, moments later the door opened and the doctor walked into the room with the technician behind him. I already knew what he was going to say before he sat down. My heart was racing. He then informed me we lost one of the twins.***

I began to cry, I was so devastated. During the rest of the ultrasound, I felt like I was in a dream. I just stared at the projection of the babies in front of me. The doctor needed to confirm that I understood that my baby was gone. He put the image of my little angel on the screen. I could see the outline of a small,l motionless baby. I looked for only a moment and then had to turn away. It is the saddest moment of my life. I was so heartbroken. I had to call Ralph from the exam room to let him know what had happened. I also called my parents. Everyone was stunned. I cried for days and not a single day has gone by since that I haven't thought about that little baby. We were so overjoyed to have two little babies after so many years of trying; it still hurts so bad thinking back on it."

Ralph was crushed by the news as well: ***"It was so hard. Were we really looking forward to having twins. It was a very rough time. We told Brock that the baby went to be with Jesus and he asked will the baby come later? There was nothing easy about it, and it added a lot of stress to the rest of the pregnancy. To go all those years of being infertile to having twins was so exciting, then so heartbreaking when we lost him."***

All of the rest of her ultrasounds checked out normally during the pregnancy. One doctor who did an ultrasound in late March 2014 spent an incredible amount of time focused on the remaining baby's heart. Jennifer began to get worried watching him. He never said anything, but he did make a recommendation to come back in less than a month. She had an unsettling feeling until her next ultrasound. She had the same doctor, and he made no mention of their last visit and did not spend a lot of time on her heart. It never came up again.

Briana Kunes came into the world on Monday, August 18, 2014 at 1:13pm. She was 8 lbs. 3 oz and 19 inches with a beautiful smile and a nice head of black hair. While the birth went without any problems this time around, the major concern began the following afternoon. Jennifer walks us through what occurred that afternoon and the devastating news she and Ralph were given: ***" I had a visitor when the doctor stopped by and told me that Briana was born with a hole in her heart called a Ventricular Septal Defect (VSD). Ironically, my visitor had a VSD as a child that had closed. I did not know anything about Congenital Heart Defects (CHD), and the doctor did not relay any more information, so I thought this was nothing serious and it would close on its own.***

I knew something was not right with Briana later that day. She would not feed. She would latch on, but fall asleep almost immediately. She would go five hours in between feeding attempts. She never ate a drop. Finally, by Friday she had lost 10% of her body

weight. the hospital said they could not let us take her home. I immediately started pumping and I fed her through a bottle.

That was the beginning of me pumping for the next 7 months. She had gained a half of percent by late afternoon! We were able to go home with a promise that we would schedule a weight check at the pediatrician's the next day. As we were preparing to go home, a doctor came in to talk to us about Briana's heart. He gave us information to see a pediatric cardiologist. Then he said, 'They will talk to about surgery options.' I looked at him and said, 'What are you talking about?' He had a very uncomfortable look on his face. He replied, 'Briana will need open heart surgery sometime within the next year.' I am pretty sure after he broke the news to us he wanted to leave that room very quickly. I think he thought we already made aware of the severity of her heart condition. Immediately after the doctor left, Ralph and I broke down sobbing trying to figure out where to go from here. "

CHD stands for Congenital Heart Defect. CHD means a child is born with an abnormally structured heart. Such hearts may have incomplete or missing parts, may be put together the wrong way, may have holes between chamber partitions or may have narrow or leaky valves or narrow vessels. It is the most common birth defect. 1 in 110 babies are born with CHD. Of those born with CHD, about 25% will require surgery. 40,000 babies are born with CHD in the United States every year.

When Briana was born, she slept 22+ hours a day. Jennifer would have to wake her just to make sure she ate. It would take her 30 minutes to drink 1 ounce. She just didn't have the strength to stay awake and eat. It exhausted her poor, little broken heart. For 10 weeks, Jennifer could feel and see every breath she took; unusually deep and rapid breaths. Her lungs were filled with so much fluid. Briana was 2 weeks old when her cardiologist said to Jennifer, "She can't stay awake because her heart is working like she is running a marathon, 24 hours a day, 7 days a week. "

Jennifer explains how she coped at that time, ***"I felt helpless and alone, but you have to just jump in and take care of your baby. It was out of my control, there was nothing I could do to change things. During that time I had to be the best mom as I possibly could be for her. I had to get her ready for surgery. I would log every ounce she drank and how long it took me to feed her. I kept track of everything, including how long she slept. I felt frustrated and uneducated at the first cardiologist appointment because I didn't know anything. I would eventually do so much research I felt as though I knew more than a first year medical student."***

With surgery looming, it was important the Kunes family felt comfortable with the doctor doing this highly important surgery. Jennifer reflects back on her first meeting with Briana's heart surgeon, Dr. Robert Stewart: ***"I first met Dr. Stewart when Briana was 6 weeks old. Briana's condition was getting worse. Her pediatric cardiologist kept increasing her LASIX every appointment and her breathing was getting more labored. She was already diagnosed with heart failure at her 3 week appointment. Her cardiologist recommended that she should have surgery within the next 6 months.***

Briana's cardiologist suggested to us that we should meet with Dr. Stewart to have him walk us through her surgery. He has a modest corner office on the fourth floor of the children's hospital. My mom and I went to the appointment with Briana sleeping the whole time in her stroller. Dr. Stewart explained everything on a big white board in his office and concluded with: "I think we should schedule her surgery for next month." I was stunned. In the six weeks Briana had been alive, we went from surgery within a year, to 6 months, to NEXT MONTH!"

Briana had the first surgery on her heart October 29, 2014, at only 10 weeks old at the Cleveland Clinic Children's Hospital in downtown

Cleveland. As a parent, you cannot mentally prepare for such a moment. It is extremely difficult, but you have no choice. It is completely out of your control. If she didn't have the surgery, she would die. You make deals with God. You pray. You cry. You hold on tight to your baby. You watch every breath. You snuggle closely and smell her newborn skin. The fear is pretty unexplainable. The moment Jennifer surrendered Briana into the surgical nurses arms, knowing they were going to stop her heart, was a pain in her heart and in her entire soul that made her feel like she would never breathe normally again.

Her surgery started around 9:00am. It would take nine stitches to sew the patch of fabric over her VSD and one stich to close her ASD. They removed muscle around her pulmonary valve to help control her pulmonary stenosis and improve her gradient. Dr. Stewart came in the Ronald McDonald Room at 1:20pm as they were closing her up. Dr. Stewart's nurse practitioner, Debbie, had been calling Jennifer and Ralph with major updates throughout the surgery on the phone set up for parents in the Ronald McDonald room. They received 6 phone calls during her surgery. When Dr. Stewart came in the room with Debbie smiling, a parent's heart flutters because you know without any words exchanged "it's done and she is ok". They had a celebratory Diet Coke for Dr. Stewart and they said she was being closed up and they would take Jennifer and Ralph up to see her in an hour.

Faith was very important to the Kunes family, and Jennifer said the rosary the entire time during the surgery. Every breath is a prayer and they had to let go of control and pray that God blessed them with a positive outcome. The praying also helps get your mind off of what seriousness you're enduring and bring your thoughts to a better place.

Ralph reflects back to those serious moments during surgery, and how tough it is for a daddy to see his daughter endure such pain: ***"It was extremely difficult to watch because I couldn't make it all better. I wish I could take the pain myself so she didn't have to have it. I***

would do anything to take it for her. It makes you feel like any little troubles in your life don't matter compared to this, when your little child is gasping for breath after drinking a few sips of milk."

They patched up her holes successfully. However, she had problems with fighting with her doctors and keeping her blood pressure up. Her body temperature was also a little low. She was sedated, had a breathing tube and numerous tubes, wires and monitors coming out of her. It was a pretty awful sight for any parent to see their loved one in.

Jennifer never left the hospital. Briana had a nurse that sat in her room watching the monitors and administering medications. She unfortunately became a monitor watcher herself. Jennifer recalls the ups and downs of the post surgery emotions: ***"Every little beep makes your heart stop for a moment. You watch the heart rate monitor the most, asking yourself, 'why is her heart rate so high?' Is it normal for that light to be flashing?***

You watch the nurse and her demeanor. I hated shift changes. Each nurse would work 12 hour shifts. I would become comfortable with a nurse and then a new one came in, another nurse that would have to break down my Mama Bear persona. Briana was extubated right after surgery and they immediately had to incubate her again. I never ask what happened; I did not want to know. Later we found out she was coming down with a cold, so I think that played a factor. To see her laying in the room with all the tubes and monitors was surreal. They warn you what she will look like and suggest you to look at pictures on the internet to prepare yourself. It prepares you on what you will see, but not how you will feel. You would do anything to trade places with your baby."

They were told right after the surgery from Dr. Stewart that he tried to remove as much muscle around her pulmonary valve as possible, but he did not want to remove too much in fear it would damage her heart. He said she would probably need another surgery in a few years; even more tough news that her parents were not prepared to hear. They thought everything would have been fixed with this one surgery. Dr. Stewart thought as she got older there might be a chance that the muscle would lessen and she would not need another surgery.

It was around this time that Jennifer heard of the Mended *Little* Hearts National Organization. She is a member of the national organization and the Northeast Ohio local chapter. She did not find this support group until two weeks after Briana's first surgery. She had felt so helpless and alone dealing with Briana's condition. When Jennifer found this support group, she realized there were so many other people out there going through the same things as her. They were feeling the same fear and vulnerability as she was. The organization helps with personal support to parents of CHD patients, but also holds fundraisers to help raise money towards research and awareness.

10 weeks and 2 days after the surgery at her cardiologist appointment, she weighed 16 lbs 3 oz. Many CDH babies can be labeled as "failure to thrive." Not Briana: her echo showed her VSD and ASD (holes in her heart) looked perfect. No leakage. She still had a mild pulmonary valve defect that would require another surgery in 3-4 years if it didn't resolve itself as she grew.

Jennifer reflects back to that moment: ***"I was so proud of her that she overcame so much. I felt hope and positivity that she was fighting so hard and winning. She was growing really well and she looked really healthy. At that time, another surgery was not even a thought in my mind."***

Because of her surgery, Briana developed Right Bundle Branch Block, which is irreversible. The bundle branches are the electrical pathways that allow the heart's electrical impulse to spread rapidly and evenly through the ventricles so that the contraction of the heart is well coordinated; basically, the electric pulses that make your heart beat. Briana's right bundle branch block is partially blocked, so she has a slight delay in her electrical impulse across the right ventricle. Dr. Stewart warned Jennifer and Ralph of this possibility. When stitching on the patch, there was chance he could hit one of these pathways. If she had complete bundle branch block she would have required a pacemaker.

Despite the early struggles, Briana kept fighting and showing she had the heart of a warrior. She was off medications at the start of the New Year. She was eating great and hitting her milestones. Jennifer, during this time, did not envy anyone else; instead these trials taught her to cherish her family's moments together. Briana's heart may have had holes in it but it was also filled with the Holy Spirit, as she was baptized on October 26, 2014, at Saint Bridget of Kildare - three days before her first surgery.

The Kunes family hoped that a second surgery could be put off for a long time. Unfortunately, that would not be the case. They found out at her cardiologist check up on July 27th 2015, that another surgery was needed much sooner than expected. Jennifer was just worried about Briana sitting still for her EKG and ECHO. Another surgery was not even a thought. The blockage around her pulmonary valve had become worse. It is called Pulmonary Valve Stenosis. They labeled it as "moderate" blockage. The blood flow going from her heart to her lungs was being restricted, and she was showing signs of pulmonary hypertension. Soon, she would start to have a blue tint to her skin. The doctors wanted to fix it before the winter season.

This was brutal news for Jennifer to hear, as she hoped it would have been several years before her next surgery. ***"I just stared at Briana's cardiologist when he told me the news. Now? Already? I vaguely remember the walk to my car after her appointment and I cried the entire way home. I was thinking that I didn't know if I could do this again so soon. The fear was terrible at night when you're lying in bed and all the what if's start to enter your mind. You do not want to think about burying your child, but you know it is a possibility.***

You just have this tremendous amount of fear. You are much more prepared and know what is coming this time, but you know it won't be any easier. We had to mentally get ourselves in that mindset again. I had so much anxiety, and it was so upsetting. It was even tougher the second time because she had this amazing personality and was walking, laughing and playing.

I did ask God, 'Why us?' many times. I was angry at times. I didn't think it was fair for Briana. Why does this beautiful, innocent baby have to endure all these obstacles? I would then have to pull myself back together and remind myself that things could be so much worse. I have my little girl that I fought so hard and so long for. People make comments that I'm strong all the time, and I kind of laugh. I have my moments of weakness. We were put in a position where we had no choice but to be strong. You do whatever you have to do and be there for your child. Even with Brock, I never wanted him to see me cry or look worried. I wanted him to know everything was going to be alright. You don't know how strong you are until you have no other choice."

Jennifer and Ralph waited a couple of days before informing five-year-old Brock his sister was going to have to go back into the hospital, because it took them time to process everything that was happening. Jennifer wanted to make sure she was strong and confident when they told him.

Jennifer and Ralph turned to each other for support. Jennifer also turned to her mother for guidance and support. Her mom is very religious and helped her get through it. She did a lot of praying with Jennifer and helped her keep at peace. Ralph turned to his sister for help and support, as she was a dietician and knew of a lot of the medical details they needed to understand.

Her second surgery was Wednesday, September 2nd, 2015, at Cleveland Clinic Children's Hospital. The surgery was once again performed by Doctor Stewart. Briana had an extremely difficult night following the surgery. All night her heart rate was elevated, oxygen saturation numbers were low, and she was running a fever of 101. She cried and moaned all night. The doctor suggested a blood transfusion. Soon after, Briana's vitals began to improve and IVs were being removed.

The hospital staff was also able to move her out of the PICU 24 hours after her surgery. They removed her chest tube a few days later and she was much more comfortable and happier. She was even able to sit up to play a little, and even took a walk around the unit. No challenge was too great or situation too big to keep Briana down.

Briana went home on Sunday, September 6th, 2015. Jennifer describes this emotional moment and the worries that came with the relief: ***"It felt so wonderful to take her home, but at the same time I was worried about her hurting herself. She had just learned how to walk before her surgery, but it was obviously still a little shaky. I knew she would be falling down a lot. Dr. Stewart put some extra wires in her sternum to make sure it would not become loose."***

Briana recently celebrated her second Christmas, and is as active as ever. She will be forced to live a life certainly a little different than others, but one that she has proven her warrior's heart can handle. Jennifer had these words of wisdom for any parent facing such an ordeal: ***"It is a hard road. You have moments of hope and despair. Panic, depression and anxiety will rear their ugly heads, and will do so with vengeance. There will be countless doctor appointments, echocardiograms, EKGs, medications, doctors, surgeons. You will not fight this battle alone. Look for support and do not be afraid to ask questions. Be your child's advocate. Admire the resilience of your baby. They are strong; so much stronger then you can even imagine. When Briana was born, we dove head first into a world that we had no idea even existed. There is never a dull moment being a 'heart parent.' Cherish every moment and don't sweat the small stuff."***

The Kunes family could teach a course on humility and courage. After a first childbirth that nearly killed Jennifer, it would have been easy for them to call it quits and only settle on one child. After four years of trying to conceive a second child and not being able to, it would have been even easier for them to give up. They didn't; they kept believing and kept praying. When they had a miscarriage, it nearly destroyed them, but they hung in there and believed in a better day.

In the first 80 days of her life, little Briana survived heart surgery. While most parents are worried about their baby possibly having colic, the Kunes had to worry about their child breathing. Less than 3 weeks after her first birthday, she had to have surgery again. This little girl is a warrior, a champion and a living inspiration and reminder of how precious and special life can be.

Chapter Three

"TWELVE OUNCES OF DARKNESS"

"A man can be a drunk sometimes, but a drunk can't be a man"

George Jones

Addiction is a battle that no one wants to or should have to fight. It's a disease that anyone can be afflicted with, as it has no prejudice against age, color or gender. There was a commercial that came out in the early 1990's that still holds true today, with a boiling egg representing a person's brain on drugs and a cold voice uttering the words, "no one says they want to be a junkie when they grow up".

For many, alcohol is seen as just as bad an addiction as any drug someone can get hooked on. It can cost you thousands upon thousands of dollars, your family, employment and, in some cases, it can cost you your life. It doesn't matter if it is hard liquor, wine or just beer; the effects are the same for those who get hooked on it, and in the end the battle becomes larger than any fight in any movie ever created. The drama is real, the effects are real and the damage can be irreversible.

No one chooses to be an addict. At first, most who are afflicted think that it won't be them, that they are stronger then the drug and the horror stories they have heard are ones that would never come their way. It doesn't take long for the dark reality to set in that no matter what walk of life you are in, no matter how much money you have in your pocket or how physically strong you are, addiction is addiction, and it will hit everyone with the same powerful punch.

How you choose to overcome it is essential, as it becomes a daily battle. Some turn to prayers, some to rehab and most choose just to ignore it and deny. For Chuck Galeti, the battle started a long time ago, but until recently his journey was never ready to be told. As he fights his daily demons and wins, his story becomes even more inspiring about a man who once had it all and lost it. Through the power of prayer and determination he has overcome, and now his story is ready to help others fighting the same battle.

Chuck Galeti was born on February 26, 1965, in Parma, Ohio, and at the age of three his family moved to Seven Hills, where he grew up. He was the youngest of three kids, as he had two older sisters. His father had dropped out of school at 16 to enter into the military and fight in the Korean War. He was a rough and tough Sicilian, but a man who loved and provided for his family.

He will be the first to tell you that he had a great childhood and enjoyed a close relationship with his father. He was a fun loving kid growing up, as he enjoyed playing little league baseball. It was playing little league baseball that led him to his first taste of success, as his team, sponsored by Chuppa Trucking, went on to win the state championship. He was even a bat boy for the Cleveland Indians during a stretch in the 1980's. Before that, his dad would take him to opening day at the stadium each year. As he continued to grow up, his love of sports remained, but he also developed a talent for playing music and played in several bands as well. He was talented and loved to live life.

For the most part, his childhood and high school years were very normal. Everything seemed fine on the surface as he excelled in everything that he did. Maybe that is why no one thought to look deeper into things. If so, they would have discovered that Chuck Galeti took his first drink of beer at the young age of 12, and he loved it! Chuck and a few of his buddies stole some wine from the Dairy Deli in Seven Hills and partook for the first time. It would eventually be the catalyst that would change everything. One moment in time would affect the next thirty five years of history.

Chuck was taught how to be a man quickly, as his father had endured a major stroke when Galeti was only 15 years old and his mother developed cancer around the exact same time. He had to provide for both of them.

Chuck continued to love both sports and music as he neared graduation at Normandy High School. He played both baseball and football and, despite his short height, he was named captain of the baseball team. With his heart and hustle more than capable of making up for his size, he excelled at football as well, as he was named an All-Conference Linebacker his senior year in the Lake Erie League.

With a successful high school career behind him, it was time for Chuck to take the next step in his life: attending the highly prestigious Baldwin College in Berea. For many high school graduates, entering college is one of the most exciting times of their lives, but Chuck could not share in those same types of happy emotions, as just a few days after he earned his diploma his father died. Shortly after that, his mother also passed away. At the age of 18, both of his parents were now gone.

He chose Baldwin Wallace because his dad was always preaching the importance of getting a good education. The message was heard loud and clear by both of his sisters, as one just retired with a Masters Degree after a successful career as a school teacher. His other sister always met with a lot of success and currently resides in Los Angeles, California.

His father never had the chance to even finish high school and always wanted Chuck to go to Baldwin Wallace, so he fulfilled his father's wish. If it was strictly up to Chuck, his first choice would have been Cleveland State to pursue a career in baseball.

With the death of both of his parents still fresh, Chuck entered college a very angry human being. He was really popular in high school but, by the time he got into college, he was very angry with the world because of what happened to both of his parents. There were times as he was finishing high school that he could hear his mother wallowing in pain in the very next room. That is sorrow and pain that doesn't disappear quickly, and Galeti took the hurt with him to Baldwin Wallace.

The pain didn't go away and, by the time Galeti was 20, the only painkiller was alcohol. This led to heavy drinking and a lot of loneliness, which then led to him having to enter rehab at the young age of just 20 years old. While most 20-year-olds are counting down the days till their 21st birthday so they could legally buy beer, Chuck was checking into Oakview rehabilitation center for an addiction to alcohol. The pain was real.

Chuck talks about this hard time in his college life: ***"My parents had died, I'm completely angry with the world and have no relationship with God because I am so lost. I didn't even know if I believed in God back then because I was so angry with him for taking my mother away. I remember lying in bed and giving a finger to the sky because my mom was screaming in the next room in pain. I would have to numb the pain with alcohol. I even went to the Indy 500 one of the last weekends she was coherent before she died because I didn't want to be around it; I wanted to drink. With no parents around and a lot of money in my pocket, it became sex, drugs and beer."***

The stint in rehab was short for Chuck; he stayed for five days and left. He didn't realize the point of going was to stop drinking - he thought that they would teach him how to handle it better. When he finally got the chance to share some of his pain with words in the groups at the center, a fellow patient started making fun of him, so he got frustrated and checked out.

Chuck was able to take some positives out of his brief stay in rehab and remained sober for the rest of his college career at Baldwin Wallace. He earned his communications degree and pointed his focus towards broadcast sports journalism. It was also during this stretch of staying clean and focused that he earned an internship with a TV station in Florida that taught him several other valuable skills, including how to handle a camera and also act in front of a microphone.

After graduation the drinking began again, but he also landed his first full-time job at a new station in Scranton, Pennsylvania. He worked overnights at the station, while also playing in a band on the weekends for extra cash. Soon enough, Chuck was asked to be a part of the morning newscast the station was starting. He liked it, so he then tried out to be the main sportscaster at the station, as well.

Things did not start off well for Chuck, however, as he got off to a very slow start and was stiff and rigid on air. He just didn't seem to have it at first, and the news director at the station was quick to pull him aside and let him know if he didn't get it together quickly, they would pull him off the air and stick him behind a camera. He was crushed and chose the worst way possible to cope with the criticism. ***"I handled it the only way I knew how, I went out and got hammered drunk! It just so happened that the company Christmas party was that same night after I got chewed out. I got smashed and it was one of those moments where I felt like I was proving a point by drinking my ass off."***

While the drinking may have made Chuck feel better at the party, the bridge he drove into on the way home did not. The accident was bad, and Chuck went through the windshield, but by the grace of God, he was okay. One cop showed up, shook him, woke him up and instead of taking him to the station and arresting him, the police officer actually took Chuck home safely. The man tried to give Chuck a break; it was close to Christmas and the officer told Chuck this was his gift. He would have his car towed to a lot and Chuck would just have to go home and sleep it off.

The next morning when Chuck woke up, his head was pounding badly from the accident and the drinking, but he didn't remember how. Upon going outside, he noticed his car was missing and instantly thought someone stole it. Not remembering anything, he called the police station and reported his car was stolen. The same cop who brought him home showed up at his house shortly after, pissed off, and explained to Chuck what happened.

Things could have been so much worse: he could have died or been arrested, and just like that his career would have been over shortly after getting started. God said it wasn't his time yet; he was given a gigantic second chance and quickly made the most of it. Chuck would return to the station, approach his job differently and much more loosely. These changes caused him to relax and perform better. He soon became one of the top talents at the station. With his new found success did not come sobriety, as the drinking continued and intensified.

Soon, his journey of success took him from PA to Youngstown, Ohio, at a station closer to his hometown. He was part of the Big Earl show at WFMJ and also the sports director at the station. As he prepared to make the jump in markets, he made the leap in love as he met and married his first wife, Dawn. He had been dating her since college and she was a calming force his life needed. Galeti figured that if he got married, it would help him quit drinking because he would have to come straight home from work each day and not have the freedom to go drink or get into trouble. He loved his wife, but it was more than love that he was interested in; he wanted to marry stability and sobriety.

He was only 23 at the time and pretty much been on his own since

15, considering that is when both of his parents got sick and he started taking care of them. It was also the last time he had stability, and that was something he craved. He also wanted to have a son because he missed the relationship he had with his dad, and he wanted to have one with a son of his own. It wasn't much longer after getting married to Dawn that their first son Russ was born in 1991. Russ was named after Chuck's father. Chuck and Dawn would later have two more children as well, a daughter Lyndsey and another son Wesley. With a wife and child, things continued to improve for the now family man Chuck as the next leg of his broadcast journey brought him home to Cleveland. Working for WKYC Chanel 3 as a weekend anchor, it didn't take Chuck long to endear himself to the viewers at home with his infectious personality and golden smile. He was ahead of the curve drastically, as most stations would require at least 3 years of on air experience. Chuck didn't have that, but he had a great work ethic and talent that could be spotted a mile away. WKYC Chanel 3 was happy to take the chance on Chuck and he proved their faith in him correct. He was only 25 years old when he arrived at WKYC. He had a bright future ahead of him and what seemed like endless happiness ahead.

Chuck was enjoying and succeeding at his new job, but as he explains it came with other pressures he wasn't at first expecting: ***"It was when I got to Cleveland that I dealt with other issues for the first time, including large egos and overall silliness. It was behavior driven by ego, and you really see the dark side of people. I'm not pointing any fingers like these are bad people, but the fact remains there are so many personalities in broadcasting that are self driven because of the pressure and nonsense involved. You have to have thick skin because people are going to say and do some very nasty things to you. Some people take things too personally. I have a personality where I'm generally friendly to people, and I was naïve as to how other people can be. A lot of people have different motives, and I can't control that.***

It is a great business, I loved it and thought it was fantastic, but it was competitive and people would do stupid things to ruin it at times for you. People are constantly bitching about it, but they don't realize how lucky they have it."

Galeti goes on to talk about some of the good people he met there that helped him at times: ***"I would have to say Jim Donovan had a good work ethic, but Mike Snynder was one of the best people I have ever worked with. Mike Synder was as classy and cool as a guy could be. One guy I spent a lot of my early career wanting to be like was Casey Coleman."***

At first it seemed like Galeti's admiration of Coleman would fall on deaf ears, as Coleman was nasty towards Galeti and wouldn't give him the time of day. Coleman had a drinking problem of his own, and it wasn't until Coleman found sobriety that the true relationship between himself and Chuck began. Chuck explains how Coleman becoming sober helped their relationship grow: ***"Once he got clean, he was an inspiration. It was night and day from his drinking days. He would pick me up, talk to me, take me to meetings and really share with me, and I will always cherish that. I remember when he got sick and was dying his spirit was still strong.***

I remember doing a story about him at his house towards the end of his life and all the guys from St. Edwards came to his house and did his yard work. I thought to myself, I hope that is me one day, having students show up at my house to do yard work. He deserved it because people liked him and he started giving back. He wasn't Casey Coleman anymore, he was a new, great guy who was happy to be sober and share his message with people. I wanted to be him one day. I wanted to grow up and be sober and do the things he did."

His job at WKYC brought him the chance to cover some incredible stories in town. It came during a time when the Cleveland Indians were a MLB powerhouse and Chuck had the honor and privilege to cover the team in the clubhouse during that incredible stretch. He got to cover them every day and be around several future Hall of Famers. Given his past history as a bat boy for the team and the opening days he attended with his father, it was a very special thing for him to be a part of.

As nice as it was to be a part of the great moments the Indians provided in the 1990's, it was every bit as tough to cover the exit of the Cleveland Browns from Cleveland in the fall of 1995. It was an emotional time during the last game at Cleveland Browns stadium, and Galeti ran alongside Earnest Byner as he took a final trip around the stadium to say goodbye to the fans along with camera man Brian Johnson.

As good as the events were to be a part of - and his high profile job helped his notoriety - it wasn't enough to help him escape his addiction of drinking. Chuck discusses how the downward spiral hurt his family: ***" I was a drunk. I loved to drink and would drink all the time. I felt horrible because when I got my second DUI in 2003, it crushed my son Russ. He had to go to school and his dad was in the newspaper for being arrested. It was embarrassing for him and my entire fault because I was selfish. I felt terrible for Russ, because other kids parents who get DUI's, they weren't put in the paper."***

The drinking also led to losing his family, as he separated from and then was divorced from his wife, Dawn. His mouth also got him into trouble when he was drunk because it led him into many fights he didn't want to get into. It also lost him a ton of money he could have spent on his family. The drinking just kept leading to many bad choices. Everything began to unravel.

Chuck Galeti felt trapped by the drinking, like it controlled him. He would always fight it, but couldn't overcome it. He was able to get sober at the age of 26 while still at WKYC and keep his past behind him for a brief stretch at Chanel 3. He tried not to hang around with any of the younger crowd at the station; he wanted to go home after the shows and be with his family. It worked for awhile because he feared losing his job at the station and his family if he fell apart again, so he stayed sober for close to four years with the help of a couple of 80 year old sponsors named Bill and Steve. He would go to AA meetings where he was finally able to stay sober. His life had changed for the better and he stayed sober for the next four years.

With four years of sobriety and a new lease on life, things were once again going well, but it would all unravel when he joined a local softball team with some friends. Chuck talks about how it all came unglued after four years away from drinking: ***"I was sober for four years at Channel 3. Things were going great, I ran five miles a day, my family was good and things were improving. It was when I joined the softball team that things stopped. It broke up a nice ritual I had going on of working, running, going to meetings and being with my family. It started off innocently and I didn't think I would ever fall back into the world of drinking, but that's exactly what happened. The team would go to bars after the game and drink and smoke pot. I thought there was no way I could crumble and return to that lifestyle, I just thought there was no way; I was wrong! Just like that, I would take a couple of puffs here and there, and then I would start drinking. It led to the next twenty years of hell!"***

His life was falling apart, his marriage had ended and things at Chanel 3 WKYC were looking bleak. He wanted out of there, as things for him just kept getting worse with the drinking. It was during this time that he met his second wife. He compared her to June Carter with his Johnny Cash way of living. Her name was Rena and she quickly became his everything. She was his party partner, his manager, a lover and a best friend.

It was during this next phase of his life with Rena that things began to unravel even more, as the partying did not stop and things got worse. He and Rena had been drinking one day when he left to go get some steaks for a cookout at their place. As he was returning from the store with the steaks, they rolled off of his passenger seat and as he went to grab them, he took his eyes off the wheel and crashed into a mailbox.

He quickly panicked: a brand new Lexus ruined, his shoulder hanging out of the socket and his third DUI looming if anyone sees. He raced home hoping no one would notice. He ran upstairs at the house and hid in the closet until the police showed up. The police dragged him downstairs, beat him up and hauled him off to jail. What was even worse is that once again the mug shot made the papers, and it crushed his kids to once again see their father in trouble.

This latest incident put him into a lot of trouble with the law. He had to check into a halfway house for awhile following it. However, like it seemed to be in his life, the drinking always cost him something, but then another opportunity was right around the corner. While seen as a blessing at the time that he kept getting second chances, it wasn't: it built up a false aura of invincibility in him that no matter how bad he screwed up, it would somehow always be fixed.

This time, it was Chanel 19 WOIO and Action News that came calling. Chuck was given the job as sports anchor and all the fame came right back to him. The sobriety he managed to maintain while in the halfway house quickly disappeared as the life of glory returned. Action 19 grew to reach high ratings, and Chuck was a major part of the success. Chuck was instrumental in covering High School Football. He even started what is called the "Friday Night Fever" style of covering it - a style other stations have copied since.

Once again, it seemed as though everything was back on track. His new wife had given birth to a two new beautiful daughters named Carmella and Frankie one year apart, and things seemed to be in order; but the drinking would not stop despite how well things were going. The drinking led to numerous things happening that he didn't agree with at WOIO 19, making them seem worse then maybe they actually were, and he decided to leave in the middle of a great run with the station.

Chuck figured that he would bounce back like he always did in the past, except this time the bouncing didn't happen as quickly as he would have hoped, and he landed at a bowling alley working behind the counter. It wasn't rock bottom yet, but he was getting closer. While working there, people noticed him and asked if he was Chuck Galeti - he denied it.

While working there, he couldn't get the broadcasting bug out of his system and decided to start a bowling show with WTAM 1100's Paul Rado. It was a great show that had good success, as it was entertaining and filled with useful facts. Galeti decided to go to Sports Time Ohio, a local cable station in Cleveland with a huge radius over the entire state including exclusive rights to the Cleveland Indians baseball games.

It was during this attempt to get the bowling show picked up by STO that God opened up another door for Galeti to walk through. Patrick Kilkenney, a producer of Indians-related programming, was at the station and noticed Chuck. Kilkenney was an old friend of his from when he was back at WKYC Chanel 3, as Galeti was there with him when he got his start. They were good friends, and Kilkenney was a firm believer in Galeti's talent. He offered Chuck a chance to host the post game call in show at the station during baseball season. It was a solid gig that would pay $300 a game and also allow him to keep his job at the bowling alley. The show would be called, "Chuck's Last Call".

Originally, the show was only supposed to be 20 minutes long, but it didn't take long for Chuck to shake things up from the original format, and it ended up being a hit. It went from being a 20 minute show that no one was watching, to a 90 minute show people couldn't turn off.

Chuck was enjoying the perks of stardom once again, as everyone was quick to jump right back on the bandwagon. Every 5,000 miles, Hyundai would give him a new car free of cost just to do commercials for them. He had clerks at grocery stores giving him free chewing tobacco and beer. He even got free McDonalds from people who recognized him.

Things were going great, it looked like everything was back on track, and then the drinking once again ruined everything. It was June 20, 2013, and Chuck had just wrapped up his show and was on his way home, hoping to get there in time to watch Game 7 of the NBA Finals between the Miami Heat and San Antonio Spurs with his wife and daughters. He eventually made it home and enjoyed the rest of the night watching the game along with drinking several cold ones.

After his wife and daughters went to bed, he left the house again, this time to head to the store to pick up a six pack of beer. He made the unwise choice to crack one open on the way home and, as fate would have it, it wasn't too much longer until a cop car was following him home. He was arrested and brought to the Parma police station around 1:50 a.m. A police officer saw him run a red light at the intersection of Ridge and Pleasant Valley Roads. Police said Galeti did not pull over right away, and when he did, the officer noticed the smell of alcohol and located an open container of alcohol in his vehicle. Galeti failed a field sobriety test and refused to take a breathalyzer inside the police station, according to police.

While Chuck fully admits he was in the wrong for being drunk and deciding to drive, he takes us exactly through what actually happened that night, a tale slightly different then what is on the record: ***"It's no one's fault but my own. No one put a gun to my head and told me to drink; it was my own choice and my own fault. The night started off innocently enough, but got out of control quickly. It was a beautiful summer night; I was heading home from Marathon with the six pack by my side. I cracked one open and took a few sips. I thought I had everything under control, I really did. I was drunk, I will admit that and make no excuses for it, but everything seemed so innocent. The beer was cold, the air was beautiful and I had on the radio and "Get Your Shine On" was playing from Florida Georgia Line. It all seemed too perfect - it was.***

I took a right on red without coming to a full stop on Ridge Road and Pleasant Valley. I see the cops light go on and my first thought was that they were going to pass me, because I didn't realize I did anything wrong. I wasn't speeding and I didn't run a light or anything. Sure enough, they pull behind me and I started driving really slow trying to get down the street and back home. The second I get out of my car, they arrest me and read me my rights.

Making matters worse, the car was gone the next day, my job with STO was gone after that, and the freebies stopped. I even got uninvited to several weddings I was supposed to attend that summer. Two weeks later my wife kicked me out, and I was completely lost."

Rena kicked him out on the fourth of July. He had no money and nowhere to go. His good friend Carmen Angelo picked him up and tried to have a come to Jesus talk with him - it fell on deaf ears. Carmen dropped him off at a halfway house, but Chuck had no intentions on sticking around and left minutes after. He then walked 14 miles into nowhere and the life of homelessness began. He was still facing jail time for his arrest, he had no money, no job and no family, but it still wasn't enough to wake him up, as the drinking would not stop.

He was at a BP station when he had a heart attack. The next thing he knew he was sitting at Metro Hospital being prepped for triple bypass surgery. The physical pain and emotional pain from the surgery where both intense. Upon checking out of the hospital following recovery, he had nowhere to go. Alcohol stole his entire life from him. One of his cousins finally took him in for a couple of months during his recovery. He then left his cousin's house and went to stay with his childhood best friend, Ron, who hadn't yet given up his partying either.

You would think that after losing 3 television jobs, two families and having a heart attack, the drinking would have stopped. The disease of alcoholism is so strong that it didn't stop - it intensified and the downward spiral continued. Chuck was convinced he would just drink until he died. It hadn't killed him yet, but he was determined to drink until it did. He even hid drinks from his wife who, by the grace of God, actually took him back in. It was his last chance at a family, but it didn't last long and, after an incident, she was gone again.

She left Chuck with nothing: no furniture, no money and just the house. He had a big screen TV, but with no money to afford cable, he was left with having to use an antenna and only pick up a few stations. With no money, he couldn't afford to pay the heat and would have to grab random items to throw in the fireplace to try and keep warm. The house had nothing else in it except beer and pictures on the wall - he had finally hit rock bottom. What little income came from washing dishes down at the corner restaurant and taking that paltry sum straight to the liquor store to buy Pabst Blue Ribbon beer.

He was cold, alone and broke; it was time for God to intervene. It was Sunday November 16, 2014, and enough was finally enough. Chuck explains the night that changed it all: ***"My son Wes had come over to watch the Browns game with me. I had nothing, it was cold, but I had my son. I was coming off a bender and we were shivering with no heat. After he left, I passed out and the next time I woke up it was three in the morning. I just started screaming! I started throwing anything I could get my hands on. I snapped!***

Later that morning I called my psychiatrist Dr. Berkman and begged for him to see me. He couldn't but said if it was serious I needed to go to the emergency room, so I did. I gathered my stuff in a small bag and chugged the last tall bay in the fridge before I chucked the empty can into my backyard and left for Parma General Hospital. I told myself, 'THAT IS IT, I WILL NEVER DRINK ALCOHOL AGAIN!'"

Upon arriving at the hospital and waiting in the emergency room, everything stopped and God came to Chuck. The time was now and the moment of reckoning had arrived. Chuck knew it was all over, he had hit absolute rock bottom, and it was time to give his life up to God. Chuck reflects back on that powerful moment when everything finally changed: ***"Right then and there a feeling of God came over me and told me it's over, your done, it will get better and I'm here to protect you."***

They took Chuck into the psychiatric ward of the hospital because he was considered suicidal. It was over, it was truly over, and Chuck didn't care; he found God in that moment and that is all that mattered. Parma transported him to Windsor Laurel Wood Center for Behavioral Medicine. Chuck stayed there for 3 days, and it helped open his eyes to so many other issues that may had been going on for years that he never even knew, such as a slight bipolar disorder. The doctors were able to get him on the right medicine to cope with that, as well.

The best medicine he had was God. He found Jesus Christ, and his life has never been the same - it has been better. 14 plus months have gone by since that awakening at Parma Hospital, and Chuck has devoted his life ever since to spreading the good word and positive message that through Christ you can beat addiction and that you're truly not alone in the fight. He was given the advice to "Don't drink, pray!" and it has not steered him wrong. The most important thing in his life is prayer, he has admitted there is a higher power and it has finally produced the sober results he has long craved to have.

His whole thinking has changed, his children have come back to him and he has let go of the pain and addiction that controlled his life for so many years. He has proven there is life after death, meaning that even though his material world of fame and material items died, his real life of walking hand in hand with Jesus Christ in a world of sobriety has just begun.

Chuck talks about his daily life now: ***"I volunteer at Holy Family and do the halftimes every night for CYO games and announce kids in finals. A big part of my time is spent on sobriety and sharing the Good news to alcoholics there is a way out."***

Chuck will be the first person to share his story and tell you that he is blessed. He realizes he could have been dead and that he could have killed someone with his drinking, but instead he lived and is now able to help others going through the same struggle and fighting the same battle. He is now leading AA meetings and helping others in need. His story is helping others on the verge of giving up. He lost everything but gained a relationship with God and, for that, he is a rich man! To keep it, you truly have to give it away.

The best way I can sum up the Chuck Galeti chapter is with the song belong:

"Feet on the Ground"

Artist WWE

"I used to fly, I used to fall, I used to hold onto life, like a fight controlling it all...

I held the prize, but I never knew how to get my feet on the ground,

I had to let go to keep hanging on, I had to run from myself if ever I hoped to be found...

I saw the light, and I heard the sound, of my feet on the ground,

Now I can still fly, and I can still run, and I'm

chasing each one of these dreams, straight into the sun...

I no longer hide, from this freedom I've

found, now I can fly with my feet on the ground."

Chapter Four

FAITH DRIVES A STICK

"I believe in Christianity as I believe that the sun has risen: not only because I see it, but because by it I see everything else."

C.S. Lewis

Kim first met her husband, Ron, on November 19, 1972, at a church in Cleveland, Ohio. They fell in love and on June 22, 1974, were married only days after Kim graduated from high school. Kim and Ron filled their home with love, and a year later they brought their first child into the world, Bernadette, and thirteen months later their second daughter, Shawna.

Kim quickly realized that having a family was a lot of responsibility, and she wanted to be the best wife and mother she could be but, not having a good role model, she knew she needed help. That help came in the form of a personal relationship with the Living God, Jesus Christ. Ron would follow just two short years later. Now, being equally yoked, they knew that there was nothing that together, God and they could not handle. What they didn't realize was how that was going to manifest. Ron explains why it was so important for him to have the spiritual connection with his wife: ***"When I married Kim she became the other half of me, but we were moving in different directions. Having the same faith moves you in the same direction."***

In July 1991, Kim was starting a new job, but had a couple days off before beginning this new chapter in her life. God had been calling Ron and Kim to begin praying daily as a couple, but they were pushing back because they were not used to praying out loud in each other's company until Kim filled those "couple days" with reading the book *This Present Darkness* by Frank E Peretti to Ron, and then there was a sense of urgency in both of them. God was calling them to pray because He was preparing them for what would soon happen and on August 19, 1991, it all made sense.

Kim and Ron both worked outside the home, so the girls were expected to help with chores, and then the day was theirs to spend either by themselves or with friends. Bernadette had just acquired her driver's license and was with three other friends in the park, learning how to drive a stick shift Mitsubishi Strada. Bernadette reflects back on the excitement of getting her driver's license: ***"I was extremely excited to get my license. To me, getting my driver's license meant freedom and maturity."***

They were on their way home and, stopping at a stop sign on a slight incline and being an inexperienced driver, she dumped the clutch, which bunny hopped them into the intersection as a 16-ton refrigerated truck was speeding down the road. The 16-ton truck hit the Mitsubishi, T-boning it on the driver's side. The impact pushed the Mitsubishi onto its side, spun it around, and made it land back on four wheels.

There were four teens in the truck: Bernadette was driving, a passenger was sitting in the middle of the front seat, another was on the far passenger's side and also a young man was in the bed of the truck. Upon impact the young man in the back went airborne, landing on the other side of the intersection in the grass. Another passenger was pushed out of the passenger's side door, and another was pushed against the door, sustaining a broken collarbone and pelvis from the force of Bernadette's body hitting into hers. The boys ran back to the truck to see if the girls were okay, and Bernadette wasn't responding. She lay slumped over with her head in her friend's lap, her eyelids filled with blood, and blood coming from her mouth and open cuts from glass down the left side of her face.

Approximately one mile down the road a police officer had a vehicle pulled over writing a ticket. A car that passed the scene of the accident moments after it happened stopped and told the police officer that a horrible accident had just happened about a mile back, which prompted the officer to leave the stopped motorist and go to the accident to access it. He saw the condition of the teens and radioed dispatch who called the local hospital, and an EMS squad arrived within minutes of the call. The EMTs determined that Bernadette was barely sustaining life and would not survive the ride in an ambulance, so a life flight was called.

Though the grace of God, Bernadette doesn't remember much of that day, as she explains here: ***" I do not really remember the day of my accident. I have two brief memories of that day, each fragmented and only seconds long. To describe the memories would not make sense. The day of the accident is pretty much gone from memory; I believe that is God's grace!"***

It takes six weeks to develop a habit. Good or bad, it doesn't matter. Do anything for six weeks straight and it becomes habit. For this family, the "prayer habit" hit its six week mark at the perfect time, as Kim explains: ***"I got a call from my youngest daughter Shawna on August 19, 1991, at approximately 3:30 p.m., while I was at work, telling me to call the police department right away. I called and got a busy signal and approximately five minutes later Shawna called me again more***

anxious, telling me the police called again looking for Bernadette's parents. Shawna said they won't tell her anything, but it was very important that they speak to her parents. I knew something had to be wrong, so I called them again as soon as I hung up from speaking with Shawna.

The police notified me that I needed to go to the hospital immediately because Bernadette had been in a serious accident and was taken there by Life Flight. I immediately called my husband at work to tell him what had happened. I was calm when asking the operator to page Ron and the whole time I waited for him to come to a phone, even though my mind was racing. I thought I was handling the news well until I heard his voice and then I started crying. He couldn't believe what I had just said so I had to repeat it, which caused me to talk louder, and this alerted my co-workers that there was something terribly wrong. One of my co-workers volunteered to drive me to the hospital, and as I walked to the elevator I felt like I had just been suckered punched. The whole thing just seemed surreal. I instantly started praying as I faced the back of the elevator. I asked God why this happened, and I sensed the Lord calling to my spirit, telling me that this 'battle' was for His glory and would be won or lost through prayer. So I said, okay Lord, you want to see a prayer warrior, just watch."

Ron explains how shocking it was to get the call that his daughter was in the hospital after a major accident: ***"The news took my breath away. I was in shock, and I just kept asking God not to let her die. I couldn't lose my daughter. I was in a panic, nauseous and nervous."***

Kim and Ron arrived at the hospital within thirty seconds of each other and were forced to face the grim news the medical staff had for them. Although, to the surprise of Kim and Ron, it wasn't a doctor or nurse that first greeted them. It was a hospital social worker, who is assigned to the immediate family for all trauma cases. The social worker ushered them to a private room, and it was through her that they learned that Bernadette had been Life Flighted to this— a level-1 trauma hospital - and she was being worked on by a team of trauma doctors. The social worker didn't know all the details and was trying to contact the police station to get all the facts of the accident. She said she would try and call the station again and asked if Ron and Kim wanted or needed anything. Kim quickly asked for a bible.

What rang in their ears was Life Flighted, a team of trauma doctors, and a social worker because of the seriousness of the trauma. They now understood why they were told to come to this hospital and not their local hospital. They called their immediate family to tell them the news and to make arrangements for Shawna to be brought to the hospital. Because of their faith, they knew that in a time of such desperation and despair, the Lord would be there with them every step of the way. They held each other and prayed. Instantly two PSALMS came to them. The first one:

" **Psalm 121**

1 I lift up my eyes to the mountains—

where does my help come from?

2 My help comes from the LORD,

the Maker of heaven and earth.

3 He will not let your foot slip—

he who watches over you will not slumber;

4 indeed, he who watches over Israel

will neither slumber nor sleep.

5 The LORD watches over you—

the LORD is your shade at your right hand;

6 the sun will not harm you by day,

nor the moon by night.

[7] The LORD will keep you from all harm—

he will watch over your life;

[8] the LORD will watch over your coming and going

both now and forevermore.

And ***PSALM 139***,

O LORD, you have searched me and known me! You know when I sit down and when I rise up; you discern my thoughts from afar. You search out my path and my lying down and are acquainted with all my ways. Even before a word is on my tongue, behold, O LORD, you know it altogether. You hem me in, behind and before, and lay your hand upon me. Such knowledge is too wonderful for me; it is high; I cannot attain it. Where can I go from Your Spirit? Or where can I flee from Your presence? If I ascend to heaven, You are there; If I make my bed in Sheol, behold, You are there... For you formed my inward parts; you knitted me together in my mother's womb. I praise you, for I am fearfully and wonderfully made. Wonderful are your works; my soul knows it very well. My frame was not hidden from you, when I was being made in secret, intricately woven in the depths of the earth. Your eyes saw my unformed substance; in your book were written, every one of them, the days that were formed for me, when as yet there was none of them.

Ron and Kim knew from those psalms that God was with them, He was their help, He was taking care of them, His love for all of them was beyond comprehension, and that he was presently in that trauma room with the doctors, nurses, and Bernadette.

The hospital chaplain brought Kim and Ron the bible and re-affirmed that they were going through every parent's worst nightmare; however, Kim was quick to correct him: ***"I said no we are not! A parent's worst nightmare is when their child is dead and they don't know Jesus Christ as their savior. I know my child knows Jesus Christ as her***

Lord and Savior; so if she doesn't make it that will be heartbreaking, but I know I will see her again one day."

After three long hours of waiting, they were finally able to see their daughter. Kim explains: ***"A trauma nurse came to talk with Ron, Shawna and I, to prepare us for what we would see as we entered Bernadette's room in the Pediatric Intensive Care Unit (PICU). She told us the condition she was in and the machines that were sustaining her life, but nothing made sense; I was in a fog, and even though I heard her words, I couldn't comprehend them. They were like forceful blasts coming one after the other.***

Bernadette had sustained a severe closed head injury and then had two grand-maul seizures after arriving at the hospital, causing more damage, so she was given a drug to paralyze her. She was hooked up to every form of life support and had a bolt in her head with a probe on her brain to measure brain pressure. Because her head injury was so severe and her brain so swollen, the signals that jump between the left and right sides were being impeded. She had a whole in her spleen and a tear in her bladder. Her pelvis was broken in four places, one of the breaks right next to her spine, and her right hip had multiple fractures. They would later find out that she had a severely deviated septum and her bottom jaw was broke through the sockets of her wisdom teeth. The nurse gave us no hope that our daughter would survive the night."

She was a beautiful young girl with her whole life ahead of her. She still had senior prom to look forward to one day. Graduation, a marriage, a family and so many other things that every young girl has every right to dream of: suddenly all of that seemed to disappear.

> *"God will not look you over for medals, degrees or diplomas but for scars."*
>
> **Elbert Hubbard**

Kim speaks about this emotional moment of having to see her daughter clinging to life in a coma for the first time: ***"As I held Ron and Shawna's hand and approached the big, solid metal door into the PICU, I felt something pulling me back and I knew I couldn't go into the room without the bible and the scriptures God had given Ron and I earlier. I will never forget how Bernadette looked, and I knew why I had that bible in my hand: it was a shield to me. She looked like road kill. I took her hand and began to share the scripture with her. She didn't respond at first, and I told her that mom was right there with her, but more importantly God was with her and she needed to fight because we were all fighting for her, and we could then see the brain waves become active. The nurse pointed out right away that she could hear us, and the brainwave response was a good sign."***

Ron explains how hard it was to see his daughter in that kind of condition: ***"It was extremely difficult seeing her that way. I had always had the ability to fix it, to kiss it and make it better for my daughters, but I couldn't this time."***

Shawna looks back at some of the ways she found to cope with what was going on around her, and how she helped keep everyone calm at times as well: "***Overall, I would say the emotions were numbness mixed with curiosity. I did not know the severity of her accident. You hear 'Life Flight' and immediately interpret that to mean severe, but how severe? I remained composed when I called my mother. I remained composed as I waited for my ride to the hospital and entering the hospital. I held composure when I saw her lying in the hospital bed hooked up to every machine possible. Her head shaved, swollen face, bolt drilled into her brain to measure the pressure, beeps and lights flashing, signals sounding.***

I listened intently as the doctors told us everything they knew to that point. I held her hand. I talked to her. I walked out when the nurses told me it was time to leave and gave a cheerful 'see you later.' **I walked to the bathroom just outside the** ***PICU, closed the door,***

fell to my knees and sobbed. That describes almost every visit I was allowed with my sister.

As Kim mentioned earlier, the medical staff was very honest with them but, because of the trauma they as Bernadette's parents were going through, nothing was making any sense. They had a dear friend, a doctor who worked there, but in the confusion Ron got his name wrong and the hospital said there wasn't a doctor on staff by that name. It didn't matter, because God was in control of this, and he allowed a meeting at a bookstore between the doctor and the church secretary who told him of the accident. He immediately left the store and headed right back to the hospital, and when Ron and Kim finished praying for God to send someone who could translate the medical nomenclature into common English, Nick was standing right there. Ron remembers, ***"He was actually able to tell us exactly what was going on. From that point on I called him Gabriel. He didn't mince words or paint a rosy picture, he always told us as it was. He let us know to prepare ourselves because every sign pointed to her not making it."***

The social worker learned quite early that they were not leaving Bernadette's side and made arrangements for them to stay right outside the waiting area in a room with a hospital bed and a chair in it. Kim and Shawna shared the bed and Ron took the chair. They would be there every step of the way to fight alongside of Bernadette. Kim relives the emotional first night in the hospital with her daughter: ***"That first night every time Ron or I felt ourselves begin to fall asleep, an unseen presence would nudge us and an overwhelming feeling of urgency would fill us, an urgency to pray. So that is what I did, silently, all night. In the morning I found out that the very same thing and feeling was happening to Ron. When we went into the PICU at 6:00 a.m., we learned that Bernadette's oxygen blood level dropped to a dangerous level and she needed an emergency transfusion; I feel it was an Angel in our room that night keeping us awake to pray because we almost lost her."***

Bernadette needed blood, so the family put out a request to the church and family members for help. So many people showed up at the hospital within hours to donate that the hospital had to send them to the Red Cross. In all of this, God worked another miracle when it was least expected. A man showed up to give blood, who thought he was perfectly healthy. Once he finished giving blood, he went into a seizure. It turns out he had a very small cancerous tumor growing at the base of his brain. Doctors found it and successfully removed it in surgery. It was one miracle in the midst of another one developing before their eyes.

When the doctors spoke with Kim and Ron each morning, the news was not good. For three straight days they told them that Bernadette would probably not wake up. They told them to start preparing for the worst possible scenario, which was death. Ron and Kim would ask the doctors what was the next hurdle Bernadette needed to clear, and then hit the phone to notify the prayer chain. While the doctors kept Kim and Ron informed, they did not give them any hope. They found their hope in God as He gave them a miracle each day, in the support of others that God sent to care for them, and in each other.

Shawna's support of Bernadette came in the form of fierce protection. In her own words, ***"I would not let anyone cry in her presence, or speak with a tearful voice. I was very aware that she could hear us. Our vocal expressions had to be encouraging. I told my great aunt Charlotte to leave her room; some would say 'threw her out.'*** **She resisted at first. I could not have her crying in there, allowing my sister to hear it. Get out. I was Bernadette's keeper.**

I would monitor her brain pressure, knowing if it reached the 30's I had to stop doing whatever I was doing. It implied brain activity that we wanted to keep low. I sang Jesus Loves Me to her and her pressure rose to 33. I stopped singing. I believe that is when she was starting to realize what was going on, while in her coma.

After waking from her coma, **I yelled at a nurse who gave my sister**

a shot. Knowing Bernadette did not like shots, I told Bernadette to look at me, as I was *on the opposite side of the nurse. I told the nurse not to warn my sister when it was coming, because she will jump. The nurse warned her, 'I'm going to give you the shot now.' Bernadette jumped. The nurse was clearly annoyed. I told the nurse how I felt about her as a nurse – I am sure it was colorful. I was asked to leave the unit."*

As the days went on, Bernadette continued to fight enormous odds. This was 1991 and well before the age of social media, but it didn't take computers and cell phones to spread the message; word spread through the power of Christ. People everywhere began to hear of the story of the young teenage girl struck by the speeding truck, and the prayers came from everywhere. It was just after the Gulf War, and United States Troops were still stationed in the Persian Gulf. Kim's cousin and another individual were there. It wasn't long that Kim and Ron received word that pockets of troops were praying for Bernadette. The local Christian radio station was notified, and a special prayer was said on the air during their noontime *Pause for Prayer* program.

> *"Sometimes beautiful things come into our lives out of nowhere. We can't always understand them, but we have to trust in them. I know you want to question everything, but sometimes it pays to just have a little faith."*
>
> ***Lauren Kate, Torment***

As prayers went up for Bernadette, God's hand of blessing came down in big and small ways each day. Bernadette was past the three day mark and still alive, and she actually began to improve. The doctors told Kim and Ron that the hole in her bladder would take six weeks to heal—it healed in 17 days, the rip in her spleen in less than that. The cuts on her face healed without leaving marks. God was present! Every single day, another miracle seemed to occur as Kim explains: ***"Everyday a new miracle would occur, including a miracle wallet at times. We had four dollars to our name when the accident occurred. People sent us all kinds of support from prayers, to food, to money, to lodging on the hospital grounds, to anything you can think of. Our needs were completely met."***

As Bernadette continued to improve, there was one major factor keeping her in critical condition: it was a high fever that wouldn't break. The doctors searched for an answer and could not find one. Bernadette was on a cooling blanket to try and break the fever, and as the family prayed the fever would come down and then go right back up. If the fever got worse, another seizure was a strong possibility, and another seizure could kill her. The doctors told Ron and Kim that the head wound Bernadette sustained was like putting a package of dried beans in a pot, covering the pot and shaking it violently.

"Ron and I prayed that God would enlighten the doctors to the problem and then we prayed that God would tell me the answer," said Kim. ***"I heard in my spirit, her tooth! Bernadette had just had a temporary cap put on her tooth and I thought it was knocked loose. I figured that there was an open gap and that somehow it was infected and that was causing the fever."***

When Kim shared her theory with the medical staff, they weren't receptive at first, some rolling their eyes at Kim, but like any good mother she was persistent and the doctors ordered x-rays. When the X-Rays where taken on her jaw, it was found that her lower jaw was broken on both sides directly though the sockets of her wisdom teeth.

With this new information, an operation was scheduled and, even though it had been over two weeks, it was a risky surgery because of the head trauma. The initial thought was that her jaw, like the rest of her body, had been healing already, so the surgeon would have to re-break it to fix it correctly. This would have required not only the wiring of her jaw, but also pins that would be fastened to a halo apparatus and put through the outside of her cheeks to hold her jaw in place. It was a gruesome thought. God was sovereign in this, too, because her jaw hadn't begun to heal at all, so the doctor didn't have to re-break it. This was yet another miracle because her body was rapidly healing in all other areas; why wasn't this one healing? ***"The surgeon said when he went in the jaw and 'snapped back into place very easily,' so all I had to do was wire her mouth shut, making the surgery quicker and less invasive than planned,"*** said Kim.

The surgeon told Kim and Ron that because of Bernadette's head injury, healing would take 8 - 10 weeks. In less than six weeks, Bernadette's jaw was completely healed. God continued to glorify Himself daily as he bestowed miracle after miracle upon Bernadette, and she jumped hurdle after hurdle.

Making things even more interesting was the fact that while the doctors worked on Bernadette in surgery, a few miles away Ron was with his family at a different hospital making the decision to pull life support from his dad who had suffered a massive heart attack. Ron had to watch his father die, and in the back of his mind worry about his daughter at that exact same moment. It was a torment no man or woman should have to endure, but the Lord knows what we can handle, even when we do not.

> *"None of us knows what might happen even the next minute, yet still we go forward. Because we trust. Because we have Faith."*
>
> ***Paulo Coelho, Brida***

Seven days after the accident, not only was Bernadette improving, but to the shock of any medical professional, she woke up from the coma. Kim describes this emotional moment: ***"It was incredible. It was***

like watching fast-forward photography. It was as if she went from being a newborn to a sixteen year old in those next moments as she began to realize what was going on. She was doing so well that the doctors brought in the speech therapist while she was still in PICU, which had never happened before."

Ron remembers fondly the night when he walked into his daughter's room to witness the miracle of her coming out of the coma: ***"On Sunday night when I went to tell Bernadette goodnight, telling her I would see her in the morning, I was holding her hand praying, and all of sudden I heard her moaning. As I looked at her she woke up - very groggy - but she looked right at me and I asked her if she was okay. She nodded yes and I got so excited that she was really awake. I told Bernadette 'to stay right there, that I was going to get mom and Shawna.' I left the room quickly to grab my wife and Shawna. It was extremely emotional and funny that I would tell Bernadette to 'stay right there.' Where was she going to go? She was still hooked up to many machines. She couldn't speak because of the breathing tube, so Kim gave her a note pad to write on and communicate with us. It was amazing that with the head trauma she was even able to write."***

Shawna was only able to see her sister twice a day during this traumatic event because of hospital restrictions involving her age. She was only allowed 30 minutes twice a day, while Kim and Ron could be there from 6:00 a.m. to midnight. God was sovereign in this situation also because just a couple rooms down from Bernadette in the PICU was a teen who had been accidently shot and, while his mother was with him, his 15 year old sister also needed something to do. Shawna became friends with this girl, and together they were able to keep each other company and provide each other comfort.

A few days after the accident, Kim asked Shawna what she did all day long at the hospital to keep busy between waiting to see her sister. Shawna explained that she and her new friend would find places all over the hospital to keep themselves busy. One such place was an alcove with a Pac Man machine. Later that day, a neighbor of Shawna's grandparent's came to visit and, after speaking with Shawna, the woman pulled from her purse a roll of quarters that she got at the bank that day. She said she had no idea why she asked the bank to give her the roll of quarters, but it became very clear after Shawna told her about the Pac Man machine. God is a God of details.

Shawna goes on to explain certain things she did to keep calm and pass the time between visits: ***"I rode the elevator. I would press all the buttons and then get off, so whoever was on would have to stop at every floor until they reached their destination. Keep in mind, I was a 15-year-old kid. I also liked to go down on the elevator. Just before the decent I would jump, causing a 'free-fall' like feeling. I kept myself busy until it was time for me to visit with her again."***

The doctors told Ron and Kim that the best case scenario would be Bernadette spending six to nine months in the step down unit before being sent to a complete-care nursing facility for the next step of rehab. They, however, did not factor God into the prognosis because within three weeks of being in the step down unit, she was playing a memory card game with a friend while the TV was playing in a room full of visitors, which the pathologist said should not be possible given the timeframe. The speech pathologist, doctors and nurses continued to tell Kim and Ron they had an amazing daughter, but Ron and Kim were quick to remind them that they had an amazing God!

Bernadette had to learn how to walk again among many other things, but instead of it taking months, it took days. In 35 days, with a fully functioning brain, she was sent home to be with her family. Her brain was actually functioning better than before the accident. Nurses and doctors were astounded by her recovery. One nurse, who had been on Bernadette's case from the first day, had the weekend off and, when he came back, told Ron and Kim he simply couldn't believe the progress in the two days he had been away. He said if he hadn't have witnessed it, he would not have believed it.

Looking back on it 25 plus years later, the family realizes clearly that nothing happens by accident in a Christian's life - including the decision to change prayers habits just six weeks before the accident - as Kim explains: ***"It was meant to be that we started praying together as a couple weeks before her accident. Since then, whenever God nudges me to do something, I almost get nervous thinking about what may be coming down the pike. I felt that God prepared us for this test by impressing on us to start praying together.***

God said the battle would be won or lost through prayer. What God calls you to do, he equips you to do. We had people praying all over the world for her. I'm positive God was with us, taking care of us not only in the hospital but outside it also. Once a week, we would drive home to look at the mail and do laundry, then drive back to the hospital. My car frame was completely rusted out and we didn't know, but God kept it together and allowed us to go to and from the hospital for those 35 days safely"

Kids who knew Bernadette through the youth group spread the word of her accident and the miracles God was working in her life. The message was so positive and moving that it motivated four young adults who had no God in their life to come to God just by hearing her story. While many kids in high school are more focused on sneaking out and doing things they shouldn't, these young adults were brought to the Lord.

Ron and Kim will tell you that there is a freedom in surrendering all to the Lord, even when it is your children. In struggles it is normal to wrestle with the Lord, but in the end it will be His will that is done. God taught Ron to let go and put it in the Lords hands and, when Ron realized this and told God, "your will be done in and with Bernadette," she began to make her turn around.

Ron explains how he came to the realization that he had no choice but to release the situation into God's hands: ***"We were at the hospital and my best buddy was with me, and I kept telling him that I couldn't let her go, she was mine and I just couldn't do it. He told me that I had no choice because she was in God's hands. Knowing he was right, I said a little prayer and told God that regardless what happens, she was his. I had her for sixteen years. I thanked God for that, and once I did that everything seemed to change and improve.***

It was exciting, and I was awestruck to see her improve and the power of God in a situation released to His sovereignty. So many people helped us and were a part of God's working plan to get us through. I think Bernadette survived because of our faith and obedience to the Lord, Jesus Christ. We are strong believers that God doesn't let anyone die before finishing the work he has planned for them on earth. Apparently he has work for her to do."

For her sister Shawna, it was a tough situation to deal with, as she was struggling to be close with her sister at the time of the accident. She admits, ***"Today, my sister and I have a very tight bond. It is made up of mutual respect, admiration and, on her side, a good amount of humor and the commonality of being annoyed by the same idiosyncrasies. We both know that no matter the circumstances, we would be there for each other if needed. We do not fight or argue. We are each other's refuge when family dysfunction reaches new levels. Bernadette and I are always on the same team. This state in our relationship took years to reach.***

We were very different in our adolescent years--far too different to get along. We surrounded ourselves with polar opposite types of people. Our bond when the accident occurred was little to none. I felt bad for her during that time. I did not understand her, why she did certain things or why she surrounded herself with certain people. I looked at her with nothing but question marks floating around

her head. To me, life seemed simple; you do your best, go for gold and nothing less. You seek out challenges and are the absolute best version of yourself that you can be. Bernadette did not take that path.

However, she does reflect all those positive attributes today. Today, I am proud to have her as my sister. Looking back, I am remorseful at how I treated her in our younger days. We fought constantly, but I always knew she loved me. "

Kim had these words for any parent involved in such a traumatic event: ***"I would tell them how important faith, prayer and hope are going through this type of ordeal, and do not get angry with God - run to Him. We need to bow our knees to him and realize that he is sovereign over the situation. A lot of people get angry with God, but it is not him that causes the pain - there is evil in the world that causes it. Too often we do not give the Lord the proper credit for the good in our lives, but we have no problem immediately blaming him for the bad. This event changed our lives and helped us realize things and situations are not important. You can replace things and work through situations; you can't replace children.***

If a parent was asked to choose between having a difficult child or having their child taken from them completely, the parent will always choose difficult over death. When we are parents, we have a huge responsibility to train our children to know the Lord, love the Lord and walk in his ways. It is a discipleship program. If our kids aren't doing what they are supposed to be doing, then I wouldn't point the finger at them. I would look at myself in the mirror, because far more is caught then taught by our children."

Bernadette survived the accident and has a very healthy life. She graduated high school with her class, went to her senior prom and did everything a teenage girl dreams of. She was able to walk down the aisle to receive her diploma without a cane or help of any kind.

Years later, she would meet her husband Bill and have three beautiful children. After the accident, all signs pointed to her not being able to have a family because of the damage to her pelvic area but, again, God had other plans, and she gave birth to three handsome boys. It meant a lot to her to become a mother, as she explains: ***"Being a mother is extremely special to me! Ever since I was a little girl I wanted to be a mama of 2 or 3 boys, and God blessed me with 3 beautiful healthy boys, who I am crazy about!"***

Today, Bernadette is very close with the Lord. However, at the time of the accident, she was still a growing teenager making mistakes and also still learning to grow in her faith, as she explains here: ***"Faith is very important! I knew God was important. He created this world and everything on it. I believed God sent his son, Jesus, to this world; born of a virgin, to live a sinless life and die on the cross for our sins. Then, three days later, He rose to life, ascended to heaven, and I believe the only way to get to heaven is to accept Jesus. However, as a teenager, I was caught up in the moment and not concerned as much with the future or, for that matter, eternity. Even though I truly believed what I knew about God, I took it all for granted."***

Bernadette has these words of advice for anyone who is forced to face such an ordeal: ***" My advice would be, get to know God on a personal level and trust Him! God loves us so much and is just waiting for us to reach out and call on Him. If we do that, God is right there and will hold and help us through!***

Romans 8:28: And we know that in all things God works for the good of those who love Him, who have been called according to His purpose."

Why did the clutch fail that day? Why did she decide to drive that truck instead of one with an automatic transmission? Those are questions may never be answered, but it doesn't matter: the real answers were provided by an unwavering faith in the Living God that proved to be stronger than any man made bond ever created. If we could learn one thing from the story of Bernadette, it is that we never know what may be coming through the next intersection, but there is no better GPS or seatbelt than faith. God doesn't care if you're driving a car, sailing a boat or flying a plane. He is always there to guide your path. We simply must let him!

> *"Do not be afraid—I will save you. I have called you by name—you are mine. When you pass through deep waters, I will be with you; your troubles will not overwhelm you. When you pass through fire, you will not be burned; the hard trials that come will not hurt you. For I am the LORD your God, the holy God of Israel, who saves you." "I know the plans I have for you, they are for good and not evil, to give you a future and a hope."*
>
> ***Isaiah 43: 1b-3, Jeremiah 29:11***

Chapter Five

WARRIORS IN PURPLE AND PINK

"That is what bravery is: to be afraid and do what you have to do anyway. You can't have courage without fear."

Tami Hoag

(Authors Note: Shortly after the completion of this book, John Venesile fought and lost his third battle with cancer. His wake, which was only scheduled for four hours, saw over 1,100 people pay their respects to this great man. He will forever be missed and loved by the lives he touched. Rest in peace, my friend.)

John Anthony Venesile was born July 13, 1937, to parents Mary and John. He was his parents' first and only child, and they were ecstatic to have him. Growing up, he did all the things normal children do: play outside and experience the world. He was relatively healthy as a child, too, with the exception of suffering from pneumonia when he was five-years-old.

One of his happiest memories was traveling to Providence, Rhode Island with his parents to visit friends. It was also his first time on a train. His Aunt took him to New York a few years later, where he visited Radio City Music Hall and got to see The Rockettes perform amongst other great site-seeing trips. He also became very close with his cousins. Being an only child, his cousins were all he had.

From a very young age he developed the passion for music while living with his grandparents. They had an old upright piano with the pedals - the kind you would pump with your feet. It also had a roll that would play its own music when you turned it on. John was tiny, so he would sit on the pedals and bounce from one to the other as he enjoyed the music. As he got bigger, he was able to reach the pedals and would pretend to play as the piano self-played. Finally, the passion overtook him, and he started taking actual piano lessons to learn how to play. Both of his parents were musical and supported his passion for learning music. His father had played the violin and alto horn in high school. His mother liked to sing, dance and whistle, and strongly encouraged John to love music as well.

He was extremely intelligent and took to his studies well. He excelled at grammar, spelling, reading and history. One of his stronger talents turned out to be typing, something not common at the time but a skill that would come in handy the rest of his life. He was a piano player, which allowed him to develop skilled hands. He won several awards for his quick typing, which peaked at over 100 words a minute. Like most who are good with words, he didn't excel at numbers at first, struggling to enjoy math and science.

His time at Wellsville High School further proved how smart he was and the thirst he had for knowledge as he flew through high school at an accelerated rate and graduated at age 16, two years ahead of the normal age. He graduated in 1954 and went on to continue to his studies at Ohio University to study Music Education. He would eventually move on and earn his masters at Case Western Reserve University.

His time there served him well, as he met his future wife Nina while attending school there. He was 16 at the time and she was 14; it was young love at its finest. He was about to enter his senior year at the time and she was only a freshman but, for John, it was love at first sight. Despite the age difference, he was still able to meet her because they were both in the marching band together. Making things more unique, both of their fathers worked on the railroad together and already knew each other.

Dating at the time wasn't really permitted in the families, so they took every chance they had to be together when they could, such as Friday Night Football games in the marching band and the parties after the games. Pretty soon, they would be allowed to start going to dances together at the school, and their love blossomed. Their love continued to grow even when he went away to college in Athens, Ohio at Ohio University to study music. John would come home as often as he could to be with Nina. Eventually on June 13, 1959, the two married at Immaculate Conception, the same church they grew up attending. The church and school have since closed, but letters have recently gone all the way to the pope asking him to re-open it. He realized his dream of teaching music following college, and started in the Independence School system. As his career went on and blossomed, he also taught in the Rocky River Schools and also Cuyahoga Community College. His fist teaching job came at Lyons School in Fulton County, a farming area of Ohio. He spent three years there, during which his wife Nina gave birth to their first child, Christopher. He loved his three years in Lyons, but they weren't without a few tough times.

Teaching salaries in the 1950's were very thin - almost impossible to raise a family on. John discusses some of the tougher times his young family was forced to endure: ***"Salaries then are not to be compared to today. When I first graduated college at Ohio University and got***

my first job in Lyons, I was only making $4,200 a year. We rented a house, but it didn't have a stove or refrigerator. Being so early into my career as an educator, I didn't have enough money or established credit to purchase one. Lucky enough for us, the local high school was getting rid of both of their old ones they had been teaching kids Home Economics with.

We were only paid once a month, and $4,200 divided by 12 months and taxes didn't leave much coming in, so we would run out of money quickly. I began giving piano lessons to high school and grade school kids for as little as $2 or $3 a lesson to earn extra money for my family. When the students left, I would leave for the store to purchase bread and milk just so I could feed my family.

The people in the town - a farming community- were also aware of our tough economical times and decided to help. They did a lot of farming and would leave fresh vegetables on our doorstep every day, directly from their gardens."

After making the best of a tough situation in Lyons, Ohio, John would eventually apply for a job teaching in the Cleveland school system or, as he called it, "the big city." He would land in the Independence school system and stay there as his career took off, and also while his family continued to grow.

John was a hard worker and loyal husband - he had no choice but to be. Not only was it the way he was raised, but he had a family to provide for. He and Nina ending up having five children: Christopher, Joel, Jonathan, Meredith and Heather. As the years went on, he was blessed again with 11 Grandchildren: Nathan, Paige, Sydney, Noah, Zachary, Lauren, Julia, Sophia, Joshua, Joelle and Austin.

Being a father and a grandfather meant the world to John, as he explains here, ***"Raising them is just like living all over again through their joy. Being a grandparent is very special to me, and I'm close with several of them. Being a grandfather to such great children is an***

award many people will never get to experience. I've been so blessed with our kids and now grandchildren."

He had a great life: a husband, a father, a large group of grandchildren and just pure happiness. He worked hard, did things the right way and treated people kindly. He deserved all the blessings that came his way, but never took any of them for granted. He kept Jesus Christ in his life as a devout Roman Catholic, even playing the organ at Sunday mass.

John explains what led him to playing the piano/organ at Sunday mass: ***"I started in elementary school because the nuns needed someone to play at mass. When you went to Catholic school, the nuns would assign you to do things around the church and you had to do it. I was taking piano lessons as a kid and was half decent at it, so it made me the clear choice to do it. I told my parents about it, and they were able to get me organ lessons to play it even better.***

Things continued to evolve as I got older and moved to Cleveland. My family joined St. Charles and I was asked to play the organ there as well, along with St. Bartholomew's in Middleburgh heights years later when we moved there. I really enjoyed it and still do! The parishioners are very nice about it and never hesitate to tell me they enjoy my playing for them."

As he taught class, he also went back to college in the evening and continued to take classes. He earned his Master's degree from Case Western Reserve in 1967 and his doctorates degree in 1992. He achieved goals in his personal life and also his career, and went on to teach for 38-and-half years. His dream was to one day retire and open a school for children to learn music.

As 2005 began, he decided retire from full time work, but still taught a little on the side because he couldn't stand to be completely away from something he loved so much. He did know, however, that it was time to enjoy retirement when he could. He started to make plans to open up his own little school to teach children how to play music when he received bad news that would change his life and end retirement just as quickly as it began.

Like often in life, even when you do all the right things, sometimes you can't control fate, and for John it was time for his biggest battle to begin. He had no symptoms of anything being wrong when he went for a normal exam with his family doctor. It was at that appointment with Dr. Mathew Walsh that everything changed. His doctor said things looked normal, but he needed to have his normal blood work done. After blood work was done, he received a call from the doctor that something was wrong because his liver enzymes were off. He was then sent for an Endoscopic exam. Shortly after, he was diagnosed with pancreatic cancer.

In 2012, pancreatic cancers of all types were the seventh most common cause of cancer deaths, resulting in 330,000 deaths globally. Pancreatic cancer is the fifth most common cause of death from cancer in the United Kingdom, and the fourth most common in the United States. Pancreatic adenocarcinoma typically has a very poor prognosis. After diagnosis, 25% of people survive one year and 5% live for five years. For cancer victims diagnosed early, the five-year survival rate rises to about 20%. Neuroendocrine cancers have better outcomes. At five years from diagnosis, 65% of those diagnosed are living, though survival varies considerably depending on the type of tumor.

Most cases occur after age 65, while cases before age 40 are uncommon. The disease is slightly more common in men than women, and in the United States is over 1.5 times more common in African Americans.

It was after the Endoscopic exam that he was told of the diagnosis while still coming out of the anesthesia: ***"I recall finding out as I was still coming to, and the news was like a punch to the face. I had to tell my family right away, because they decided that I see a surgeon at the main campus of the Cleveland Clinic who specializes in Pancreatic cancer."***

John was stunned by the news. He was in disbelief and nearly fainted when hearing it. As usual, his wife Nina was by his side and vowed to be his biggest support - they encountered the battle together. When he told his family they were devastated and shocked, but positive as the Venesile family was strong. They were a family built on love for one another and faith in God.

The official diagnosis was Stage 2 Pancreatic Cancer followed by surgery, radiation and chemotherapy. The only surgery available to attempt to remove the cancer in his pancreas was called the Whipple procedure. The Whipple procedure, also known as Pancreaticoduodenectomy, is the most commonly performed surgery to remove tumors in the pancreas. In a standard Whipple procedure, the surgeon removes the head of the pancreas, the gallbladder, part of the duodenum (which is the uppermost portion of the small intestine), a small portion of the stomach called the pylorus, and the lymph nodes near the head of the pancreas. The surgeon then reconnects the remaining pancreas and digestive organs so that pancreatic digestive enzymes, bile, and stomach contents will flow into the small intestine during digestion. In another type of Whipple procedure known as pylorus preserving Whipple, the bottom portion of the stomach, or pylorus, is not removed. In both cases, the surgery usually lasts between 5-8 hours.

Following the surgery, the chemotherapy worked but wrecked havoc on his body. He took more than a year to recuperate and caught C-Diff while in the hospital, which increased his stay for nearly a month longer. He was also constantly tired, couldn't eat anything and lost 30 pounds.

John relives those horrible sacrifices he had to make while getting chemotherapy treatments to stay alive: ***"Chemotherapy has devastating effects on your body. Each treatment got harder and did more and more damage to my body. After my surgery in 2005, I began chemotherapy and radiation. After the surgery I lost 30 pounds, and it took me a year to recover and regain my strength. I started going***

back to the gym and doing things to eventually get my weight back to where it started before I got sick."

While many who have experienced cancer can only see the negative side - and very understandably so - John tried hard to take a different approach: ***"Perhaps at first I found it as a death sentence, but then I found that prayer and positive thoughts from family, friends and myself soon gave way to hopefulness."***

His family remained his pillar of strength through the horrible ordeal. Pancreatic cancer is a death sentence for most, but John and the entire Venesile family refused to stop fighting and never gave up hope. Finally, in late 2005, after months of pure hell, he received the news he had worked so hard to hear: the cancer had been beaten and he was in remission. His heart, head and soul were filled with emotions of thankfulness to God and his family for seeing him through all that he experienced.

John reflects back on how he handled the good news of being cancer free: ***"It was incredible news to be given that the cancer had gone away. I immediately thanked God. I strongly believe in the power of prayer and its ability to produce miracles. The feeling of being cancer free is like lifting a house off of your back."***

Anyone who has ever beaten cancer can tell you that the fear of it coming back never truly goes away. It was fear that John would now be faced to live with everyday going forward. In 2007, he had a large scare when a lesion was found on his right lung. Once again, he leaned on his faith and was blessed when a surgeon performed a successful lobotomy to remove it. He would eventually heal, but the worst was still yet to come.

In 2013, nearly ten years following his first bout with cancer, it returned to his pancreas. It was found through a routine CT Scan. The hell he had to live with in 2005 had reared his ugly head yet again. This time there was no surgery or radiation, as chemotherapy was needed right away.

It was devastating news for John to hear, as the cancer had returned. He explains what he turned to the second time around for strength: ***"Once again I turned to family and prayer for strength. I often wondered how people fight cancer when they are single and have no family or spouse. I don't know how they are able to do it, because I have had my full family support. My wife watched everything I ate and made sure it was all organic. My kids kept me going. I was so crushed and couldn't look into plans for recovery at first so my kids did it for me at first. They did a lot of research to help me."***

It was during this time of research that a new miracle experimental drug called Tarceva was found that helped John keep the cancer at bay. ***"I was on a experimental drug for nine months in recovery that I only found out about because of my kids' research. It was costly, but the Cleveland Clinic found a way for me to get the drug for practically nothing, and it really helped me. My family and grandchildren have all been so loving and supportive and always want to see me get well."***

Once again, John and the Venesile family were ready to battle for the patriarch's life. Through chemotherapy, nutrition, exercise, faith in God and strength in family, he beat cancer again. He found out he beat it the same way he found out he had it: through a routine CT Scan.

John was lucky enough and blessed by God to beat cancer twice but, while he was blessed with two miracles, he saw some who were not. ***"I joined an organization called Pan Can, which is a group that supports those who suffer from pancreatic cancer. I made a lot of friends who also suffered from the same cancer I had in this program. Some were getting better, but some were worse off than me. I was to become very close with them and all of their families and now, sadly, they are all deceased.***

I also saw it in my church with people who suffer from cancer. They would admire how I was able to find the strength to still make it to church and play the organ, even when I wasn't feeling well.

Sadly, several of those people in my parish who suffered from cancer have now also passed away.

I have lost a lot of friends, and I often stop and think about them being gone and why I am still here. I think it is because I want to help other people and that I believe in prayer. I believe that miracles do happen, and they have happened for me."

John had these final words to share with anyone who suffers from cancer or has a family member or friend suffering from this horrible disease: ***"You have to be your own advocate when it comes to your body. You have to know your body and not let the doctors tell you what you're going to do, but rather have some kind of a voice in that. You have to have a support system. You have to have friends and family, and you have to let them help you because a lot of times when you're facing a deadly illness people do not know how to approach you. You need to reach out to people for help and let your family help you. Most of all, you need to pray. You need to turn to God and ask him what he is planning for you and how he is helping you. Prayer is just not for you, but for all the people who are suffering. When I did my chemo, I could not believe how many people were there getting treated in all ages, races and gender. Stay off the internet and don't read the doom and gloom pages. Don't stop your life!"***

As said before, cancer has no prejudice on gender, race or religion. It is an evil that effects lives all around us and attacks when no one suspects it. There is no way to avoid it, but stories such as these will explain how, with spirit and belief, you can fight and beat it!

On December 28, 1957, around 8:10 at night, Eugene and Geraldine Hawkins gave birth to their eldest child, Catherine. Cathy was just the first of what would become a big family, as she went to have sisters Nancy, Gerie Linn and Sherrie, along with brother Ben. When Cathy was six years old, her parents got divorced. Her mother would later remarry and have two more sisters, Charlotte and Lora, along with a brother named Charles - all younger siblings would join the Hawkins kids.

It was a packed house, as Cathy had seven siblings living with her. It was also a moving house, as she lived everywhere on the West Side from Sackett Ave to Clifton. Between the times she was a small child to the time she was 18, she had 7 different addresses in all. Her mom was her hero, as she saw how gracefully her mom took on eight kids, raising five of them on her own for almost five years and then taking on three more under the age of six. Her mom held the house together and found a way to feed everyone even during lean times.

Her stepfather Charlie was another hero of hers for taking on five kids and teaching them hard work, responsibility and also how to have fun. There was no money to do things, but he was the big kid of the neighborhood, playing kick the can and all kinds of other fun games to keep everyone entertained. She also looked up to her grandma Hawkins, who was a strong, kind woman who always had toast and chocolate milk for all the kids at every visit.

She was the oldest of five kids, then the oldest of eight kids. She took care of the kids, taught the little ones to read, cleaned and shopped. She even handled the laundry duties of all ten people. In her very little spare time, she loved to read. She would always have her nose in a book for as long back as she can remember. She even carried "extra" books to read that were not required by the school when she was at school to read between classes.

Her ability to be responsible combined with her love of reading allowed Cathy to excel in Junior High School. She was in honors classes in Junior High School, and it gave her the opportunity to go to John Marshall High School to take advanced classes. She was originally scheduled to go West Tech High School, but this gave her the chance to go to John Marshall with four of her friends, who were also part of the honors program. They were bonds that remained for years, one of which is a close friendship she has to this day.

She graduated in 1976 and attended the very prestigious Baldwin

Wallace College in Berea to study. So determined to attend and excel at college was Cathy, that she took a bus everyday from her house in Cleveland to Berea. She excelled at college and graduated in 1980 with a degree.

Baldwin Wallace is one of the top schools in Ohio for academics, and is highly regarded around the country as well for producing top scholars. With that kind of pressure to perform in a stressful environment, along with being in a house of ten people, most people would have cracked. However, Cathy continued to excel. In a packed house it is tough to find a quiet spot to study, but Cathy explains how she made things work for her when she needed moments of solace: ***"There were times when I really had to study for an important test. I would go up in the attic and be by myself. I would find the quietest spot and just be by myself so I could concentrate. Plus, I loved to read, so I was able to mentally escape when I needed to. I also loved being outside in nature; it really helped calm me. Sometimes I would ride my bike from Cleveland to Berea and make stops along the way with my books so I could study. I loved studying outside. That is the way I kind of got through stuff."***

It was while she was attending college she met her husband, Chris. They were taking American Indians class together in January of 1977. They sat next to each other, and Chris would often bring the newspaper to class with him so he could do the jumble puzzle. Cathy liked Chris right away and would watch at the window to see if he was coming to class each day. She would get excited and anxious waiting for his arrival each time to class on the third floor.

Chris was living on his own at a house in Lakewood and would work at Don's Fish Market in Rocky River at night. Despite working in River, living in Lakewood and going to school in Berea, Chris still made time for Cathy, and their love grew. They got married after college was completed and were excited to begin their life together. They would soon move into an apartment in Fairview Park.

It was about three years after graduation that Cathy found out she was going to be a mother. She wanted to work with children following college, but ended up working for the Navy Finance Center and really enjoyed her job when she received the news about the pregnancy. Chris was working in construction at the time. Cathy and Chris loved to attend the county fair, and that is when Cathy took the opportunity to tell Chris they were going to be parents. She was excited but nervous, with all the normal questions new parents have. Am I ready for this? Are we ready for this?

Even with the nerves of becoming new parents, Cathy remained ecstatic at the thought. She always wanted to have kids since she was a little girl. Taking care of kids, brothers and sisters was natural to her, as she began babysitting at the young age of ten. With siblings and step siblings, she was a natural to it. Chris and Cathy would go on to have three children total: Katie was born in April of 1983, Chad in December 1986, and Ian in February 1989.

It was a relationship with her oldest child, Katie, that was truly rewarding for Cathy. Katie was always interested in singing. The Wade family had begun going to church after a neighbor invited them one weekend, and Katie began singing in the children's choir. She was also interested in ballet, then baton. As Katie got older, Cathy would begin to take her to competitions out of town, including some as far as away as Dayton, where the state competitions were held.

Katie was also involved in the Riverside Singing and High School Choir, which took them all over the country for her choir performances. They were held everywhere: in churches, schools, outdoors events and anywhere with a stage. Cathy enjoyed every second of watching her daughter sing, and it only got better when her daughter reached high school. It was during high school choir that Cathy had the chance to be a chaperone on a choir trip to Disney World. Cathy loved every note that came out of her daughter's mouth with only the pride a mother can have, as she explains here: ***"It was the most amazing experience to hear that girl sing. It often reminded me of my childhood when I sang in choirs. I often teared up in pride watching Katie perform. She wasn't always the best traveler because of motion sickness on buses, but I didn't mind taking her in my car separately."***

As the spring of 2000 arrived and Cathy started to get excited about her daughter looking at colleges in the coming months, and as Katie was set to graduate the following year, her life was met with sudden shock. Things began to unravel when she attended a routine mammogram in March of 2000, only the second one she ever had at the age of 42. She could sense something was wrong when they put her in another room by herself for what seemed like an eternity.

After nearly an hour by herself with no one coming back to speak with her, she became almost positive something must have been wrong. It was only a short while later that her fears came true when two nurses came back to speak with her and informed her that they found a lump and that she most likely had breast cancer.

The news didn't catch Cathy by complete surprise, however, as she had a few warning signs the previous November: ***"The previous November I reached across my body to grab a book off the bed. My right arm pressed against my left breast and I thought I may have felt something. I sat up, felt around and found nothing. I don't believe I thought about it again until after I heard that I most likely had breast cancer. I was nervous and scared at first. I was alone in that room forever and had not even redressed after the mammogram. They tried calling several doctors to confirm it, but for some reason they couldn't seem to get a hold of anyone. I was numb for quite awhile after that. I didn't tell my family at first until a later biopsy confirmed their suspicions."***

Cathy was full of questions and wanted to get as much information as possible before telling her husband Chris what was going on. She wanted to be sure before she started worrying everyone. When she eventually told him, it was on a walk in private - an emotional moment. It wasn't until after she was completely diagnosed that Chris and Cathy sat down with the kids and told them, as well. The kids were sad about the news but very supportive, two of them getting tattoos later in life in support of their mom.

One small bit of good news was that they caught the cancer early enough to do battle against it. It was in stage two and the tumor was two centimeters. The first doctor Cathy went to see did not work out. Her friend, who had cancer, recommended her doctor for Cathy, but it wasn't meant to be as the connection simply was not there. Cathy was wise not to settle because cancer treatment has to be with someone in which the patient has full trust in.

A short while later, Cathy found another doctor, this one much more to her liking - she found the Diaz practice. It was a small private practice of husband and wife. They did the removal surgery of the lump and then chemo and radiation all in their office. They were good people who even traveled to foreign countries to donate their time and service. Dr. Diaz was so proactive with Cathy's cancer that he did the biopsy on her first visit. He was kind, and so was his staff; it made Cathy feel very at ease being there during such a tough ordeal.

After the results came back from the biopsy with Dr. Diaz, she had to go for another even more in depth biopsy. Chris was with her this time, and he also liked the Diaz practice and supported Cathy's decision to go with them moving forward for treatment. Surgery was scheduled to take place a few days later at St. Johns Hospital to remove the lump and six months of chemotherapy to follow. The surgery was in March 2000, and the two-centimeter-long lump was removed. He also removed the sentinel lymph node under her arm. This is done to check if the cancer cells have escaped out of the area and possibly have moved into the rest of the body.

Dr. Diaz did things different then most doctors. He only had Cathy come in for chemo once a week following the surgery with the last week of the month off, so it was three straight Mondays with the fourth Monday of every month off for rest. It was not the normal at the time, but he felt doing things a bit different would produce better results and not be so hard on the patient having to go through it.

Chemo is hell for anyone to have to go through and affects everyone differently. Cathy talks about some of the challenges she had with it: ***"The worst was losing all my hair. As I started the chemo I was told it would happen, but it did not happen right away. I would go in for the chemo and still have hair. I really wasn't feeling too sick just yet. After the early round of sessions, my husband would take me to a nice restaurant down the street and I started to believe that maybe I wouldn't get sick and lose my hair. The nurses assured me I would.***

It wasn't until the last few months of chemo that things starting getting very bad. One day in the shower two handfuls of hair came out, and then that's when it really hit me that I had cancer. It hit me that I really was sick and could die. It was a devastating day, as it really hit me that many people die of cancer every single day. It thinned quickly after that, and I had to start wearing a wig when I was out in public. My children were very supportive and knew how to cheer me up. They even offered to shave my head for me. I let them!"

Wearing a wig was anything but fun, it was torture and embarrassing for Cathy, who was a naturally beautiful woman with the kind of smile and energetic personality that would instantly light up any room she walked into. This was a woman who spent her life nurturing and taking care of others. She was a woman with a heart of gold and a nature about her that anyone would like. She was just a good person in every which way, and she was about to do battle in the fight of her life, for her life.

People tend to say stupid things every single day, but when someone has cancer a silly remark can become downright cruel. Cathy was already sensitive enough and a bit insecure about having to wear a wig and ball cap everywhere she went when someone at church said something awful to her. The woman, clearly oblivious to Cathy's illness mocked her and poked fun, accusing Cathy of only wearing a wig to try to look young and hip. Cathy was forced to endure the ignorance of others no matter how un-deserved it was.

One thing - like with anyone who had to go through chemo - Cathy began to notice was the things she once took for granted were disappearing. She normally had an unlimited amount of energy and could go all day long from work to home to whatever she had to do at night and never got tired. Suddenly, because of the chemo, that once unlimited supply of energy was gone.

No matter how bleak things looked, Cathy refused to give up hope and kept together her incredible spirit. ***"During the whole ordeal, I kept saying I can do this. It was the only time in my entire life I had ever been sick and in the hospital. I never had broken bones, sickness or surgeries. I just said, ok, this is my one thing and I will get through it. I really never had anything go wrong in my life, so I told myself I could handle anything once. Even though I had cancer, I still kept the attitude that I was going to do this one time and be done with it. My family had no sickness in it, and I just knew I could get through it once.***

I relied on a lot of support from my friends Maria and Don when I didn't want to burden my own family. I have never been one of those people that need people to feel sorry for me and do things for me. Don always knew how to cheer me up and gave me a boost with kind words. I didn't tell a lot of people about my cancer at my church even, because I didn't want people knowing and feeling sorry for me. I tried not to rely too much on my immediate family, either. They loved me for sure, but I didn't want my cancer to be a burden on their life."

Even with a positive attitude, chemotherapy and cancer takes its toll on everyone. Cathy began to struggle at times from fatigue and sickness but tried to keep a positive outlook and began to think of what may happen to her children if she did die. It was then that she came up with a goal in her mind to cope with things. ***"I did worry about what would happen to my children if I died, and my new mission became making it through to the point where they were all done with High School. I just wanted to get through all of it and be able to be there to see them graduate. Please let me be their mom until they are at least 18!"***

The positive attitude - along with the support of her husband Chris and chemotherapy - began to pay off, and after nearly 8 months of chemo the results, determination and courage began to show. It was in late September that Dr. Diaz gave Cathy the good news that the chemo worked and the cancer appeared to be gone; however, just to be on the safe side, he highly recommended six weeks of radiation. Cathy was not thrilled at the prospect of radiation but, after months of chemo, she was a warrior and knew that she could handle radiation, even if it was five days a week for the next six weeks; she saw the finish line and began to sprint towards it.

Cathy expounds on how helpful the support from her husband was: ***"Chris was my biggest support and cheerleader. He would always tell me I had a nicely shaped head, so I would go without a wig because he didn't feel embarrassed being around a bald woman. He made me feel nothing less than I had always been. He was so kind and loving and did anything he could to make me feel better. Everyone with cancer should have a person like him in their life."***

While she was going through this she found some solace in a support group at the Moll Cancer Center on the second floor. There was a very nice woman named Patty Coravelli that ran a great support group. It was a wide variety of women who had suffered with or from cancer. Some of the woman had it 20 years ago, and some found out they had it only

20 hours earlier. It provided a wide variety of support and experiences to share in. It also had a resource library available to everyone, as well.

As Cathy was defying the odds and beating cancer, she became friends with a fellow cancer patient in her cancer support group that didn't make it. Cathy talks about this hard reality that the disease could kill good people with bright futures ahead of them: ***"I met a woman named Cathy, spelled the same as mine. I remember she was making a quilt blanket for her daughter, who was only six years old. I still have her number in my phone book. I remember that quilt she was working on. After she died, it was too hard for me to come back to the meetings, so I stopped going. The worst part for me was the fact that she had a six-year-old daughter. It was just too hard to imagine and cope with the thought of that little girl growing up without a mom."***

On December 29, 2000, after nearly a year straight of hell and suffering, worrying and angst, Cathy Wade was cancer free. She did not go out and celebrate, she simply thanked those who helped her and tried to get back to normal life. She felt wonderful that it is was done, but was simply anxious to return to her life. Millions of people die from cancer every year; Cathy beat it!

She didn't regret what happened to her, she was just glad to be done with it. She went to all her checkups over the next five years, as cancer patients are obligated to do. Her cancer had been estrogen-filled positive, so they put her on a pill for the next five years that was supposed to prevent the cancer from returning. It worked - it didn't return in those five years. The pill was called Tamoxifen.

Hormone therapies slow or stop the growth of hormone receptor-positive tumors by preventing the cancer cells from getting the hormones they need to grow. They do this in a few ways. Some hormone therapies, like the drug Tamoxifen, attach to the receptor in the cancer cell and block estrogen from attaching to the receptor. Other therapies, like Aromatase inhibitors, lower the level of estrogen in the body so the cancer cells cannot get the estrogen they need to grow.

Treatment with the hormone therapies Tamoxifen and/or Aromatase inhibitors lowers the risk of breast cancer recurrence, breast cancer in the opposite breast and death from breast cancer. Hormone therapies used in breast cancer treatment block hormone actions or lower hormone levels in the body. Although these drugs are called hormone therapies, they act as "anti-hormone" therapies. By contrast, MHT is meant to increase hormone levels in the body to treat menopausal symptoms.

After five years, she had the option to stop taking the pill, as it was no longer obligatory; she chose to do so. Never did she ever think it would return: it was 2006, and she had been healthy for the full five years. She had full confidence that her one time with this horrible disease was done, she had beaten it, and it was time to move on with life. One year later, it returned.

Earlier tests led doctors to believe that the re-occurring lump was scar tissue and not a cancerous lump. After the more in depth testing was done, it was found that, in fact, it was cancer.

Cathy details how she found out it had returned: ***"I was going for diagnostic mammograms every six months and everything always seemed fine. One day I was out to lunch with my friend when I reached across the table to grab something and my right arm pressed against my left breast and I felt a lump. Amazing, unbelievable, I couldn't believe it. I passed it off until I got home and was able to really check it out. It is not easy to feel with a regular breast examine: I had to be sitting up, not laying down to feel if there was anything there. It is how the doctor examines you, laying down.***

Dr. Diaz had just retired, and when I called they recommended his replacement. I didn't say much, but just made the appointment and went in to see the doctor. The new doctor said I was fine, then scheduled me to come back in six months. I couldn't believe he couldn't find the lump, so I grabbed his hand and placed it on my

breast where the lump was and asked him, what that was? He didn't say anything, I don't think he could. He added a cancer blood test to my prescription and left the room. Needless to say, I never went back to him."

Why did it return? She had already gone to hell and back, she thought the worst was over and that the rest of her life could begin. It was enough to break the spirit of anyone, but Cathy refused to lose; she had beaten it once and she was determined to beat it again. It wasn't easy at first, however, to think that way, as Cathy explains the battle she had in her mind with God after finding out it returned: ***"I think I would be lying if I said I wasn't angry with God at the start of the second time around. Regardless of how much a person goes to church or how much they believe, at some point we all ask, why is this happening to me? The first time, not so much. I didn't think about it too much. I still went to church every Sunday, taught Sunday school; the whole thing, the first time around. The second time, not so much. I really wasn't going to church much at that point. I learned a lot of spirituality and a lot about Mother Mary from my friend Maria that helped me get through a lot. But the second time, yes, I was angry.***

Sometimes I think that God was trying to teach me a lesson with the first time I had cancer, and maybe I just didn't get it, so it was given to me again, almost like a hammer over the head. What didn't I learn the first time, that I needed to learn the second time? That is what I thought."

The plan of attack was different the second time around. Dr. Diaz was retired, so instead of going to the small office in Westlake, she began going to the extremely large Cleveland Clinic Main Campus near downtown Cleveland. It was a 45 minute drive from her house, but the longer drive was a small price to pay to win round two in the battle for her life. Cancer may have returned, but Cathy was ready to fight!

The other big difference was that radiation would not be an option this time around, but the doctors did have a few tricks and options up their sleeves. This was in 2007, and the medical profession was starting to have both breasts removed - even the one without the cancer in it. Cathy had a choice to do that, or just have the one removed with cancer and have it replaced. She chose to just have the one with cancer in it to be removed.

Under certain circumstances, people with breast cancer have the opportunity to choose between total removal of a breast (mastectomy) and breast-conserving surgery (lumpectomy), followed by radiation. Lumpectomy followed by radiation is likely to be equally as effective as mastectomy for people with only one site of cancer in the breast and a tumor under 4 centimeters. Clear margins are also a requirement (no cancer cells in the tissue surrounding the tumor).

For most women, lumpectomy has a good cosmetic result. In rare cases when a larger area of tissue needs to be removed, lumpectomy can cause the breast to look smaller or distorted. There are types of reconstruction available for both lumpectomy (if there is significant distortion) and mastectomy. If you need to have a large area of tissue removed and two breasts of matching size are very important to you, you and your doctor will need to decide which surgery is best for your situation.

During lumpectomy, the surgeon removes the cancer tumor and some of the normal tissue around it (called the margins). A pathologist looks to see if cancer cells are in the margins. If there are cancer cells, more tissue needs to be removed until the margins are free of cancer. Ideally, this is all done during the lumpectomy, but analyzing the margins can take about a week. So, sometimes after the pathology report is done, the margins are found to contain cancer cells and more surgery (called a re-excision) is needed.

The surgery done to Cathy required fat to be taken from her stomach to make the fake breast, so it was almost like getting a tummy tuck along with a new cancer-free breast. It was a risk she was willing to take to get rid of the cancerous breast. After her surgery in July of 2007, the recovery was eight days before she could come home, then chemo began again. It was a familiar nightmare for Cathy, but one with a previous happy ending she was determined to see again.

Her estrogen was causing the cancer cells to keep reforming. After she was done with chemo the second time and it appeared that once again the cancer had left her body, she met with her OBGYN to discuss options on how to regulate her estrogen. The OBGYN was able to recommend one of two things. The first were a year's worth of shots called Zoladex, or Cathy could go with option two, which would be removal of the ovaries.

In premenopausal women, most of the estrogen in the body is made by the ovaries. Because estrogen makes hormone-receptor-positive breast cancers grow, reducing the amount of estrogen in the body or blocking its action can help shrink hormone-receptor-positive breast cancers and reduce the risk of hormone-receptor-positive breast cancers coming back (recurring).

In some cases, the ovaries (and usually the fallopian tubes) may be surgically removed to treat hormone-receptor-positive breast cancer or as a risk-reduction measure for women at very high risk of breast cancer. This is called prophylactic or protective ovary removal, or prophylactic oophorectomy. Removing the ovaries is one way to permanently stop the ovaries from producing estrogen. Medicines also can be used to temporarily stop the ovaries from making estrogen (called medical shutdown). Ovarian shutdown with medication or surgical removal is only for premenopausal women.

Cathy opted to have the full Hysterectomy surgery instead of the year's worth of shots. It was a tough choice to make but, as with everything else, Cathy handled it like a champion: ***"My OBGYN, she made a great point. She asked me if I was planning on having any more kids; at 50 years old, I wasn't going to. I had cancer twice already, my sister had***

cancer too, so why take any chances? She made a lot of flipping sense, so I agreed to have the Hysterectomy because it made the most sense. She also did a great job with the surgery and, even though it was a major surgery, it was the easiest of all the ones I had to endure."

At the point of beating cancer the second time, they never truly say that you are cured. They just keep up with the six-month mammograms. If you can make it to five years the second time, it looks like the statistics will be in your favor that it won't return. Cathy took Arimedex then Letrozole for the first three years following the surgery, as it was supposed to have the same effect that the Tamoxifen did the first time.

It has been 16 years since Cathy was first diagnosed, and 8 years since she beat cancer for a second time. She is a true warrior and an inspiration. She learned along the way that not everyone was as lucky as she was, as she lost a close friend along the way who also suffered from cancer, as she explains here: ***"The one person I lost whom I was close to that died of breast cancer was my friend and co-worker, Debbie. She got her first bout of cancer just before I got my second one. We had worked together in the past - sporadic through almost ten years, but intensely - daily for weeks at a time when we worked together. She taught me a lot about the best part of my job, and we connected personally on various aspects of our family live. We had - and were - going through some of the same struggles. We talked out many issues over the years, and I believe gave each other ideas, support and a sounding board.***

I know it took her a while to call me and approach me about her breast cancer. I don't believe we really touched on it that much over the years, and she is a private person like me. Of course, when she finally called to ask and possibly discuss it, I assured her that she could and should ask any and all questions. She had a few good friends and relations in the medical field but, as we all do, needed to talk to someone would was/did go through it, not just medical people.

We talked many times. The biggest thing I assured her of was the fact that you need to be comfortable with all of those medical people who are and will be caring for you, providing and deciding on your treatment. She found one doctor she liked, but her family wanted her to go to a 'higher up,' more well renowned specialist. I told her I felt that one of the main reasons I got through that harrowing year (2000) was I liked and felt comfortable with my doctor, his staff, and the room where I was given the chemo. I did talk to another doctor (as everyone should) and made my own choice. I think that helped and she chose the doctor (woman) that she was most comfortable with.

Of course, then we moved on to the funnier, smiling, side of cancer. Losing your hair- I gave her my wig and she was looking forward to trying out lots of them, all hair colors and styles! I was not that adventuresome, staying with mainly the one, mostly just wearing a hat or nothing at all. I was told I had a nicely shaped headed, so I often went bald at home. The family was fine with that, and who cared about the neighbors! It was summer time for me, May to September. I had quite a variety of baseball caps that the family had picked up for me.

Debbie's cancer returned in December of 2012. I remember her calling in January, trying to find a way to ask me to donate some leave time to her. She never really came out and said the cancer had returned. Mostly we talked about the holidays and, by now, she had a granddaughter whom she loved to brag on. The girl was very smart and already an 'adult.' Then she told me about the pain in her back and how her husband had to call the ambulance for her.

But she down played everything and never mentioned cancer. I don't even think it dawned on me, she sounded so good. Of course I donated 2 weeks of leave to her: she was the major bread winner in her family and needed the money. I think we talked one more time briefly that month. Then, in March, a coworker called and left a

message that Debbie had passed away. I know I was in total shock. I never realized that she was that sick and the cancer had returned. I got more of the details from the coworker later on.

Of course, as time went on, it really sank in. Her husband decided no funeral, no wake, nothing. There was a very small family dinner that no friends were invited to. So there we MANY of us who loved Debbie, worked with her over the years, and had no real way to say good bye. There was no get together to reminisce about how great and kind and helpful a person she was to all.

That, of course, got me thinking at times. What if it comes back? What if I die an earlier death before my mom, siblings, husband and grandkids? What do I want (funeral/wake) after I am gone? What do I want people to remember about me? And I believe - at those times especially - I would look at what I was doing, how I was treating people. Was I taking enough time with my friends/family instead of working all the time? Did I write a note, or sent a text or give a call enough? My job was/could be all consuming. I was always thinking about the next thing that needed done, 24/7. By then all the kids had scattered the country, so it was me and the husband. I was no longer the mom, constantly worrying, trying to fix, caring for kids, cleaning up, giving advice not wanted. There was less laundry, cooking, shopping. I needed to try harder to stay connected to them and my extended family. There was always more that I could do. Was I doing enough? What if?"

Even with the doubts and worries about the future, Cathy has always been smart and intelligent enough to realize how much divine intervention she had along the way both times. She has always been appreciative for the two miracles God gave her. Cathy had these words for those who were there to support her along the way both times: ***"I just want to say thank you for being there! I also want to say thank you for those of you who didn't make such a big deal about it and***

didn't pepper me with constant questions. For the people who didn't dwell on it, thank you! I loved the cards people sent me, they were great and I was able to read them at my leisure and they really helped. In fact, I still have them! Some people just randomly sent over pizzas and gift cards. That was so incredibly awesome of people to do that. Thank you for not dwelling on it and not making it the large Elephant in the room."

Cathy Wade was the oldest of five, then the oldest of eight. She has always been a self reliant person who never asked anyone for help. She was never a whiny person, she did things on her own and always had a "just do it" attitude. So when you really think about it, did cancer even have a chance against her?

Cathy looks back at the whole experience and realizes it was her husband who played a large part in getting her through: ***"My husband was there for every doctor appointment, every chemo treatment, and was always my cheerleader. It took courage and strength on both sides - not just mine, but also his."***

Cathy's husband Chris played a large role in helping her during both bouts with cancer. He made her feel special and helped her laugh and feel loved in tough times. Cathy kept the following quote on her mirror, because it was the way her husband made her feel: ***"Promise me you'll always remember: You're braver than you believe, and stronger than you seem, and smarter thank you think! You are an amazing person!"*** It was a quote that Christopher Robin said to Pooh.

Both John and Cathy have been lucky enough to survive from their battles with cancer. During the writing of this book, I posted a request for anyone who had lost a family member or friend to cancer to leave their name on my Facebook page and I would post their names in this book in loving memory. To my shock and sadness, it only took minutes for the page to fill up with names that have been lost to this horrible disease called cancer. May the following names forever rest in peace:

Eva Panagopoulos:

Pat Hehr

Amy Bilyk

Elizabeth “Betty” Morgan

Alice Galeti

Sarah Bankston

Ramona Taylor

Mary Joyce

Mary Margaret Perpich

Helen Parsons

James A. Mahoney, senior

Paul A. Mahoney

Thomas O. Mahoney

Josephine DeLuca

Bob Moore, Jr.

Michael Joseph Bensi

Judy Dean

Laura Cury

Thomas Ineman

Robert Alan Mick

Kevin Matthew Neenan

Guy Chester Little

Debbie Davis

Merelene Zahnke

Charles “Chico” Sandru

Margaret Anne chamberlain

Bruno Pell, Sr.

Bill and Barb Gardella

D.F. Coyle

Evelyn Blumena

Ronald Hagen

Dolores Corson

Pilar Rodriguez

Paul DeLuca

Geraldine Boyle

Monika Chmura

Nora Amoroso LaChance

Scott Meng

Joanne Vicarro Kodrin

Leo McNulty

Therese Kunes

Julie Rich

Larry Lacey

Dave Kintop

JoAnne Gedeon

Walter Trzaska

Stanley Trzaska

Femi Olajide

Sara lynch

Joan Mancino

Maggie Gastaldo

James Gillespie

Andy Still

Djordje Soc

Shirley Ashbrook

Archie Pickett

Anne Omilanowski

Bill Brennan

Jean Margaret Pepp

Chapter Six

THE MIRACLE IN MONTREAL

"The human body experiences a powerful gravitational pull in the direction of hope. That is why the patient's hopes are the physician's secret weapon. They are the hidden ingredients in any prescription."

`Norman Cousins`

Most little girls grow up dreaming of marrying their prince charming and having children and living happily ever after. Sure, some dream of being movie stars, athletes, and music stars, but at the very root of it, they dream of being normal. To live a life full of dreams and happiness is the common goal. No one ever dreams of being sick, let alone developing an illness that can be crippling. For every school dance that maybe didn't go just right or every boy who forgot to call, there was someone out there with even bigger problems and challenges. This is the story of that girl, one who only wanted to be normal and loved. Sadly, a crippling illness called epilepsy almost took that away from her forever.

Maria McKee was born August 15, 1956, at Marymount Hospital in Cleveland, Ohio. The name Mary would forever be linked to the new born as the date, August 15, is the assumption of the Blessed Mother Mary and the presence of the blessed mother of Jesus would forever be a strong force in her life. Maria would be taught from a young age the importance of Mother Mary. Her Roman Catholic background also helped instill the importance inside of her as well to worship the Virgin Mary.

Maria was born into what would become a large family, but one never short on love. Her parents Joe and Rosemarie DeLuca had met in high school and fell in love. In fact, Joe uttered the words, "I'm going to marry that girl," upon setting eyes on her for the very first time. They went to school at John Adams High School and, even after Joe's family moved to Bay Village at the beginning of his senior year of high school, he kept dating Rosemarie and their love for one another grew.

They got married soon after high school, and Joe was drafted into the Army during the Korean War shortly after their wedding. It wasn't long after Joe left for war that their oldest child Josephine was born. It would be six months before he saw his first born daughter for the first time. Joe would eventually return home from the military, and the DeLuca family grew from there. Maria was the third born to Joe and Rosemarie DeLuca. Her older siblings - Josephine a sister and Peter a brother - came before Maria. Joe and Rosemarie would go on to have five more kids following Maria - brothers Joseph and Jimmy - along with sisters Rosemarie, Frances and Anna. It was a packed house with plenty of action. Because of the ten people living under one roof and the DeLucas being a one-income family with father Joe working as a postal worker, money was always tight, but love and fresh baked bread was always abundant.

Maria's life started a few hours later then maybe it should have, as the doctor was late arriving and, despite Rosemarie being fully dilated, the nurse urged her to hold the baby in. She was ready to come into the world, but the world was not yet ready for her. The preventing of her life arriving was the start of lifelong issues she would be forced to endure. Because of the pushing back of the baby, by the time it was time for Maria to arrive, the doctor needed to use forceps to get her out, which caused brain damage. It is not common, but in her case it happened and it would be the beginning of major concern. It caused brain tissue to be scarred; she was fighting an uphill battle minutes after being born.

As Maria grew up very early on, she had a few seizures as an infant. Not many, but when they did happen the doctors referred to them as febrile seizures. They most commonly occur in children between the ages of 6 months and 5 years. This was believed to be the case with Maria. It was common, and the doctors and others never thought to look further into it. A febrile seizure is associated with a high body temperature, but without any serious underlying health issue. The reason why it wasn't looked into right away was because most seizures are less than five minutes in duration and the child is completely back to normal within sixty minutes of the event. Long term outcomes are generally good with little risk of neurological problems or epilepsy.

Simple febrile seizures do not tend to recur frequently, and do not make the development of adult epilepsy significantly more likely compared with the general public. Only about 1% of infants who suffer from frequent febrile seizures go on to develop severe epilepsy as adults. Sadly for Maria, she fell into that 1%.

For Maria, the warning signs of epilepsy would go past febrile seizures as she grew past her toddler years and became a little girl. She would begin to wake up in the middle of the night with full body muscle spasms in her arms and legs. This is more commonly known as "charlie horses" and can become quite painful. She would wake up in the middle of the night with intense pain and scream in agony, waking up the entire packed house. Her mother would run in and rub her legs down, work out the cramps and do whatever she could to comfort her daughter until she was able to lay back down and fall asleep.

When telling the doctors about her muscle spasms, their solution was to increase potassium in her diet, so Maria would start each day out with an orange and banana. It didn't help, and the daily pain continued to intensify.

Life was different for Maria growing up for obvious reasons, and she didn't know why early on. She just knew that she was different then her older sister Josephine, and teachers didn't hesitate to remind her. As the third child of eight, she was always asked by the teachers why she did things so differently than her older siblings Josephine and Peter. She was trying to find her way, and not knowing the full extent of her issues just yet, life was very hard.

Maria didn't realize she had epilepsy yet, but she knew something was different and wrong growing up. The other kids realized something was wrong as well, as she had several classmates in kindergarten through sixth grade that would tease and pick on her. The teachers were uneducated at the time about the illness. They didn't know how to recognize signs of it and treated her like an outcast instead of offering her help. In fact, teachers could actually be the biggest bullies back then, as Maria explains here: ***"The teachers would yell at me and call me a dummy. They would put a dunce hat on me when I had the seizures. I could have a seizure triggered by something as simple as the school bell going off. It could even be a light switch being flicked on or off, or any sudden movement that could set one off at any moment.***

It was horrible, as I instantly bit into my tongue and mouth during the seizures and felt extreme electric shocks of pain. My brain would just go into its own world and I all I could hear was the last sound of the lights flashing on and off. I felt like I was spiraling down a tunnel and couldn't control it or make it stop."

Instead of understanding, the teacher would just stand there and yell at her to stop until the horrible ordeal was over. Her classmates, at first in shock, would eventually start getting used to it and begin to laugh at Maria during the seizures. This could happen up to ten times in a day when you factor in all the bells ringing throughout the day and all the times a teacher would flick a light switch on and off.

It got so bad early on that every time a loud or sharp sound would go off, Maria would fall into that deep dark place of agony by herself. It ravaged her body so badly that most times the seizures would cause her to pee her pants, and she would have to wear soiled clothes for the remainder of the day until she returned home from school. So scared of ever having a full bladder, Maria would skip drinking anything at lunch or at anytime throughout the school day. She was so desperate to hide things that she would purposely sit in the mud or a puddle in the schoolyard to cover up an accident that had just occurred in her pants. She resorted to wearing several layers of underwear on most school days, hoping that it would soak up her urine before others could see it. It didn't always work; most times the urine would still soak through her clothes, which only led to more name calling and harassment from her classmates.

The seven years between kindergarten and sixth grade were the worst of her life. At the time, the seizures were small but, without anyone knowing what was wrong with her, she became awkward, scared and alone. She didn't feel accepted and was scared every single day when she woke up.

Despite all the sadness in her life, Maria was starting to develop a hidden talent for drawing and artwork that no one saw yet, she explains here: ***"The one thing I loved to do was draw. But back when I was young, and only the smart kids were allowed to take the art classes because it was seen as a bonus. My grades struggled because of the seizures, so I was never allowed to take the art classes I wanted to be a part of so badly. Because of this, no one knew I could draw so well.***

Not even my parents or seven siblings. It was hard because my father was an incredible artist, and so was my older brother, Peter."

When Maria had a project that consisted of any form of artwork for her other classes such as History or Science, she would turn in incredible work, but the teachers would fail her because they did not believe it was her doing the work, instead insisting it was her brother Peter or her father. The teachers refused to believe the beautiful work was coming from her. Maria would offer to prove it by drawing something right there on the spot, but the teachers wouldn't even allow that. It wasn't until many years later when she had children that her aspiration to draw was fulfilled, as she was given the chance to draw for her two sons.

As Maria continued to grow up, things began to increase in difficulty at a different level. She started "womanhood" early, getting her first period at the age of 11 years old. Ironically enough, at the same time, her mother was in the hospital getting a hysterectomy, as she had just had her eighth child and was done having babies. Because of her menstrual cycle beginning, this caused a new type of seizure to begin. This new seizure was referred to as a Temporal Seizure.

Temporal Lobe Epilepsy is a chronic neurological condition characterized by recurrent, unprovoked epileptic seizures which originate in the temporal lobe of the brain. The seizures involve sensory changes - or a memory disturbance. The most common cause is mesial temporal sclerosis. Temporal lobe epilepsy (TLE) is the single most common form of partial seizure. The causes of TLE include mesial temporal sclerosis, traumatic brain injury, brain infections such as encephalitis and meningitis, hypoxic brain injury, stroke, cerebral tumors, and genetic syndromes.

It is important to note and understand that ***"Temporal lobe epilepsy is not the result of mental health disorders or fragility of the personality."*** Or, to put it into simpler terms, it has nothing to do with how someone lives their life, how their personality is or anything they do; they are stuck with these and it could happen to anyone - it doesn't make them an outcast. Anyone who sees it that way is mis-informed and close-minded. People can't help it that they have seizures, and for others to laugh at them for it is sick and inexcusable.

Maria did have some hope as she entered sixth grade. It was junior high and kids from other grade schools would be joining her at West Drop Junior High. These were kids who didn't know her and may not judge her, meaning she actually had a chance to make a friend, if not several.

Helping matters for Maria as she reached Junior High was the fact that older brother, Peter, was very popular because of his great artistic ability, a three-sport star athlete and had good looks. Peter had made the DeLuca name proud. Another reason why he was so loved was because of his very kind heart. Those plans of sudden popularity were dashed, however, with the signs of epilepsy still not detected and without her teachers being able to understand how to treat her. Maria was moved to the special classes for troubled kids. She was mixed in with students who were very bad, and others who were labeled slow, handicapped and almost a lost cause. Maria was neither slow nor stupid, but she was unfairly labeled because of a condition she couldn't control. All of these classes were located in the same hallway, and the other students would refer to it as the dummy hall.

It was during this stretch, however, that Maria finally had a breakthrough. She had eighth period English taught by Mr. Lawrence Frye. He would change her life, as he not only taught her how to properly read, but also was the first person to truly recognize that something may be wrong beyond her control. He saw something in Maria's face during a seizure that until then had gone unrecognized. Mr. Lawrence had a family member with epilepsy, and knew exactly what was going on with Maria.

He was the first teacher that didn't yell at Maria for being bad; he understood what torture she was being forced to endure. He was very understanding and was the first person who finally alerted her parents to what was going on and the serious problem she had. This was only two weeks into the sixth grade school year, and Maria would now have to miss many days of school because her parents were able to get her in with brain specialist's doctors to begin treatment.

The doctors began to treat Maria by asking many different questions to find out exactly how bad it was. She would enter Fairview Hospital to begin a series of tests, one of which was a very painful and scary procedure called a spinal tap.

A spinal tap is used to collect cerebrospinal fluid to confirm or exclude conditions such as meningitis and subarachnoid hemorrhage, and it may be used in diagnosis of other conditions. The patient is usually placed in a left lateral position with their neck bent in full flexion and knees bent in full flexion up to their chest, approximating a fetal position as much as possible. The area around the lower back is prepared using aseptic technique. Once the appropriate location is palpated, local anesthetic is infiltrated under the skin and then injected along the intended path of the spinal needle. A spinal needle is inserted between the lumbar vertebrae L3/L4 and L4/L5.

The patient would often be asked to lie on their back for at least six hours and be monitored for signs of neurological problems. Patient anxiety during the procedure can lead to increased CSF pressure, especially if the person holds their breath, tenses their muscles or flexes their knees too tightly against their chest.

Side effects during the procedure arc serious as well. Some side effects include spinal or epidural bleeding, adhesive arachnoiditis and trauma to the spinal cord or spinal nerve roots resulting in weakness or loss of sensation, or even paraplegia. It can also result in perforation of abnormal dural arterio-venous malformations, resulting in catastrophic epidural hemorrhage. Removal of cerebrospinal fluid resulting in reduced fluid pressure has been shown to correlate with greater reduction of cerebral blood flow among patients with Alzheimer's disease.

The doctors sat Maria in a high chair with the back open and strapped her arms and legs down so tight she couldn't move them at all. Her head was placed in a helmet-like contraption and she couldn't move it, either. They proceeded to put needles into her back that went straight through to the vertebrae in her spine, draining fluid from it. They then put in syringes filled with dye, which they proceeded to also inject into her back. They even told her it was okay to scream because they knew it would be extremely painful.

After the spinal tap procedure was done the next text consisted of Maria being curled into a little ball and carted into the ex ray room for another series of x-rays. After that, she was wheeled back into the room for a short period of rest.

Maria was stubborn; she didn't want to give into the pain and didn't want anyone knowing how bad it felt. Instead of screaming, she asked for a wash cloth and bit down on it as hard as she could to avoid screaming. Shortly after the testing was done, she was diagnosed with epilepsy. She had never heard of it, but her father Joe did as his cousin suffered from it.

Back then this was such a dark cloud that most people didn't share that they had it, and many families would try to ignore it. The DeLuca family was very different; they loved Maria and began to adjust life for her condition. Maria's parents were very loving to their whole family, and didn't treat her different. They shared her story with other families in a way to spread the message and look for a cure.

Maria was blessed to be a part of the DeLuca family that sat 10 to a dinner table every night. Father Joe took care of all of them on a Postal Workers salary. The family knew of hard times, but also knew how to love one another. Despite the condition, her parents did not keep her from doing things she wanted to do. They let her help with chores around the house - with eight kids, there was never a shortage of beds to be made or rooms to be cleaned. Her mother didn't hesitate to teach her how to cook, something Maria would love to do. They allowed Maria to run, jump, ride a bike, do all the things kids do; they didn't want to keep her in a bubble despite how serious things were. They allowed her to have a childhood under a caution, but none the less a childhood!

Her parents did their best to keep things positive for Maria because when they sat down with the doctor, it was nothing but bad news. While he never took the time to explain what Epilepsy was, he didn't hesitate to tell the DeLucas all the things Maria would never be able to do or achieve in life. It wasn't a short list.

1- The Doctor told Maria that her family would grow to be ashamed of her and more than likely put her in a mental hospital.

2 - He stated that Maria would never be able to operate a vehicle and never obtain a drivers license.

3 - Sled riding was out, bike riding was out, any form of fun for a child was out. Everything from cheerleading to jumping rope was out.

4 - He explained how she would never have a boyfriend, get married and she could forget about having children. No man would ever want to be with her, and if for some reason she found a man, giving birth could and would kill her.

Maria was young, naive, and taught to respect her elders. She was under the impression that if a teacher or doctor said it, then it would have to be correct. However, she was also stubborn, strong willed and wouldn't allow anyone anywhere to tell her she couldn't follow her dreams. She made a promise to herself that one day she would drive a car and get married. She was too young to realize how babies were made, but by golly, she would figure that out, too. No one on planet Earth was going to tell her she wouldn't one day become a mommy. For the next decade, Maria would see this doctor and hear about all the things she would never accomplish, and for the next decade Maria did everything she could to prove him wrong!

Maria explains the dynamic of the bad news given regularly in the doctor's office at each and every visit for close to a decade: ***"At each visit he reminded me of all the things I would never be able to do, but never once talked about the things I could do. He never gave me confidence or showed faith in me that I could do something. He insisted that I would be a nothing, and accomplish nothing. He told me not to even try at anything, because I wouldn't be able to do it and it would just hurt my feelings when I failed.***

This man put me in tears so many times until one day when I told him that unless Jesus, Mary and Joseph come down from Heaven and tell me I can't achieve anything, I won't believe him. He was not happy to hear this and reminded me that he was the only person who could help me and that I would have to follow his rules exactly."

These checkups would continue every three months and most times, Maria would be in the cold waiting room, wearing nothing but a thin paper gown waiting hours for this man to come in and exam her. He would never explain anything or even give coping techniques; he would simply ask how many seizures she had since her last visit and proceed with his exam. He wasn't looking for a solution as much as he was just monitoring it.

It was very uncomfortable for Maria because the exam process entailed her to have to walk back in forth in front of him wearing a gown that did not close in the back. The exam also called for him to touch her in all of her nerve endings, including the ones in private areas. Making things even more uncomfortable for the young woman was that he would have her bend over and touch her toes, while he probed areas that had nerve endings - a humiliating exam for anyone to have to endure, let alone a young scared girl.

Maria goes on to explain just how uncomfortable those exams were: ***"He was the doctor, so I did what he told me. I did not like what went on in the exam room, especially the touching of the private parts. I***

never told my parents what he did to me and where he touched me. Looking back at it today, I wish I had told them about the touching. You just didn't question adults back then, you were told to obey them no matter what they told you to do.

Each time when the exam was over, he would call my parents into the room and add a new prescribed drug for me to start taking. When I returned home from these visits, the first thing I would do is climb into my bed, pull out my bible I received for my first Holy Communion and read it cover for cover, then pray the rosary until it was time for dinner."

The seizures would get worse as the years passed. Maria was lucky, however, that she had the same teachers all through junior high school. She loved them because they understood her and knew how to handle her. They knew how she felt and what she was going through. Junior high only lasts three years, and eventually she would have to graduate and start high school at John Marshall. It was a school whose reputation would become synched with the DeLuca name in the sixties and seventies because of the outstanding athletic performances of her brothers Peter, Joey and Jim. Peter would finish second in the entire state of Ohio in the 1973 in Wrestling. He was also a three sport letterman and captain in Football and Baseball as well. Peter could do it all.

Despite her strong family presence in the school, Maria was still afraid because it meant new classmates, new teachers and new challenges. Sadly for Maria, her fears became justified as the seizures became worse - much worse as they developed into the dreaded Grand Mal seizure. This is a form of Epilepsy characterized by tonic-clonic seizures involving two phases: the tonic phase in which the body becomes rigid, and clonic phase in which there is uncontrolled jerking. Tonic-clonic seizures may or may not be preceded by an aura, and are often followed by headache, confusion, and sleep. They may last for mere seconds, or continue for several minutes. In more common terms, they are large and dramatic, and there is no way to ignore them or hide them. It stops your entire day, and sometimes puts a person out of commission for several days.

The bullying got worse in high school because of the dramatic seizures. Maria would describe them as feeling like her brain was on fire and her whole body was being electrocuted. She would end up biting her tongue during the seizures and her eyes would roll back in her head. Her entire body would fall to the floor and go into a large uncontrollable spasm.

It is one of the most horrible sights anyone can ever have to witness. Her arms, legs and head would bang into whatever was near them. She would also lose control of her full bladder. The worst part was that while all of this was going on, she was aware of what was going on and couldn't do anything to stop it. Students having to witness this would scream in fear at the sight. Sadly, the sounds of fear from the classmates would also be accompanied by the sounds of laughter. The students would stand around calling her names as she was flopping on the floor in need of someone to hold her down so she wouldn't get worse hurt. She would often black out, waking up minutes and sometimes hours later in the nurse's office. She would change her clothes into dry ones, then have to go right back to class. The other students would snicker at her as she walked to her next class. She was praying that the bells would not set off another one as she walked.

The school would eventually realize that they needed to adapt to the situation at hand and figure out a safe area of the school they could bring Maria to before each class was over and the bell rang. That way, in case it caused a seizure, there would be people there ready to help her. Sometimes it worked, sometimes it didn't.

One person who stood by Maria's side in school was close friend Patty Lynch. Patty helped Maria when she was down and stuck up for her when others would put her down. Patty even threw Maria a surprise 16th birthday party. It was an act of kindness that Maria has never forgotten.

Against doctor's orders, Maria tried out for the JV cheerleading squad at John Marshall. She knew the dangers at hand and that the doctor told her she would never make an organized team, but she was never one not to try something she truly believed she could do. Her doctor wouldn't even allow her to take gym class. Maria was determined to prove him wrong and begin fulfilling dreams.

The day of tryouts came and she nailed her entire routine during tryouts. She did everything she had to do to make the team and performed well. Just as she was wrapping up her routine during the tryout, she went for a cartwheel. During this process the school bell rang and she went into a seizure mid-cartwheel. She was lucky enough to be on a padded matt and to come out of the seizure quickly but, still scared and embarrassed at what happened, she ran out of the gym and ran the entire four mile trip home in her wet gym clothes.

Later that night Maria received a call that was step one in proving the doctors wrong, and also her first step towards achieving multiple dreams in her life. She reflects back on that moment here: ***"The way they told you if you made the team was by having a varsity member girl call your house and give the good news. Well, in our house the phone ringing was a terrible thing because it could set off a seizure. Every time the phone would ring, one of the other nine people in the house would run to it as soon as possible to answer it. My siblings would go as far as to tell people not to call the house if possible, but with ten people living under one roof this was almost impossible.***

The phone did ring that night, and it was a girl that my brother Pete was going steady with. She was also one of the varsity cheerleaders. She told me that she had good news for me, that I had made the team! It was an incredible feeling that my hard work and determination had paid off. The girl was also nice enough to let me know she grabbed my purse and school books I left behind in the gym

when I ran out. All that didn't matter; I was a real cheerleader and no one could ever take that from me."

Maria was not even close to being done with breaking down barriers, yet being a part of such a large family on one income meant that having a part time job in high school was a must. Once again the doctor had told her active employment was not an option, and that her being a productive member of society was next to impossible. Maria was bound and determined to get that part time job and help her family anyway she could.

In the summer following her tenth grade year of high school she started working for Riverside Nursing Home as a nurse's aid. She loved the job, even as hard as the physical labor was. There was no bell ringing every hour and the one phone they had was at a front desk with a very soft buzz, not even a ring to it. During the weeks she would work as an aid after school and on Sundays they had her in the kitchen cooking. It was a small nursing home with only 38 patients, but Maria relished the chance to help others.

Some of the patients really didn't need to be there, they just had nowhere else to go. Some would come in for rehab but never leave, as their family left them there to die. This did not matter to Maria because she loved and cared for all of the patients. It soon became a family affair as her older sister Josephine became a nurse there, as she was in nursing school at the time. Her brothers Peter and Joey were working there part time as janitors and her sister Rose was washing dishes.

One of the most vivid memories, and one that would also affect her life, took place one faithful Christmas morning: ***"My first Christmas working I was upset at first, because who would want to be away from their home on Christmas? But I was still happy to have a job and understood the way it worked. They had the women without children work the holidays, it made sense. I walked into the room of my favorite patient, Mary, and when I reached over to roll her over I***

realized she was dead. She was one of the 16 patients under my direct care and I froze in fear. I felt responsible and began to cry right away. I started praying as well for her, and then went into a seizure. Luckily it was one that only lasted maybe 20 seconds. I dropped to the floor, meanwhile the other patient in the room is screaming for the other nurse. By the time the nurse got in there I was able to pull myself back up to my feet, but I was soaked in urine.

My coworker was not thrilled with the scene she walked into. She told me to go get changed and come right back to help get Mary ready for the morgue. I did exactly what I was told to do and came back as quickly as I could. As I walked back into the room I was surprised to find three other patients in the room, up, dressed and already eating breakfast.

My brother Peter, who was also working that day, came in and got them ready for me while I was changing. He was not supposed to, or paid to do so, but his heart was so big he couldn't help but help."

When she wasn't working or cheering, she still wanted to pursue her love of art. As she sat with the school counselors, she pleaded with them to let her take art classes. The school refused to bend on their rules and continued to tell her that she couldn't take art classes because she wasn't smart enough. The other fear was that with all the sharp objects in an art class someone could get seriously hurt if she began to seize. Instead of art class, they did allow her to take cooking class, which made little to no sense because, despite her love of cooking, it was odd that the school would encourage her to be around hot boiling pans, sharp knives and hot ovens. It made little to no sense, but she made the most of it.

In her first three-plus years of high school and all the preceding years before it, Maria never had a boyfriend. Guys didn't date girls like her, girls who were unfairly labeled retarded. The boys were pleasant to her in groups, but didn't want to be alone with her in case she might seize. Some guys would ask her out, thinking that she would be so desperate for male attention that she would instantly have sex with them. They quickly discovered she was not that kind of girl and moved on. No matter where she was, if she was put into that type of situation with a guy, she would instantly leave and walk away no matter how far from home.

It was around this time that some of the boys in school would begin a cruel joke that no person anywhere should have to suffer through, let alone a young woman with epilepsy. A random senior in high school would ask Maria out, take her to a nice restaurant and then skip out on the bill and leave her to pay it and walk home.

Maria explained how this horrible joke was able to take place: ***"I was at a party one time, and this guy asked if he could take me out the next weekend. He seemed nice enough, so I said yes. He would pick me up and take me to the Brown Derby, which was a nicer restaurant at the time. He left right after desert came and never returned to the table. Shortly after, the waitress would return to the table and hand me a note from him that said, "I got you, retard!" It also had the bill with the note. I was lucky I always kept enough money in my purse just in case. I paid the bill, left a tip and walked home in tears.***

I remember the first time it happened. I got home merely a half hour after I left and my mother and sisters were wondering why I was home so early. I was so embarrassed that I told them I had a seizure and excused myself from the date; I was too embarrassed to tell them what really happened. It was so bad. I would cry myself to sleep as I was reading my bible again.

To this day I wonder who would do such a mean thing to someone. It would happen a few times more to the point if someone came to me at a party or game and asked me out, I just started telling everyone no."

That would all change when she met Don McKee. He was the star wrestler at rival High School West Tech and had graduated a few years prior. Don had come from a broken home and did not have the best of reputations. Don fell in love with Maria instantly but, because of how many times she had been hurt in the past, Maria was unwilling to even entertain the thought of speaking with him.

Maria talks about her first impressions of Don: ***"I had known who he was. He was three years older than me and had graduated from our rival high school West Tech. He had a bad reputation as a tough guy who would walk around in all leather. They were called Greasers back then. The girls he went out with from Marshall didn't have the best reputations. I was nothing like anything of these girls he went out with. To be honest, I just wanted him to leave me alone at first because I was afraid of him. But God had a plan, and it was his will for it to happen."***

Maria did make two friends who would become two of her best friends for life. One was a girl by the name of Camille Bensi. Camille was a cute Italian girl who never made fun of Maria. She met Camille through her best friend, Sue Hehr. The three of them did everything together, and they were true friends.

With prom on the horizon, she still had never been asked to a dance. If she went to a dance, she would just stand behind the punch bowl and watch everyone else have fun. With prom around the corner and Camille being the nice person she was, she wanted to see Maria go to a dance with a date, especially prom. Camille offered to let her boyfriend take Maria. It was a kind gesture for Camille to make, but there was one problem with the plan: her boyfriend was Don McKee. She hadn't been dating him too long and was unaware of his crush on Maria.

"Sue called me up one night and told me that Camille felt bad I didn't have a date for prom, and if I wanted to borrow her boyfriend for the weekend I could. Why was she letting me have him and not Sue, who also didn't have a date? Well, as luck would have it, it was Don McKee. I guess he heard Camille telling Sue I didn't have a date and quickly volunteered himself. Camille, the nice person

she was, lent me her boyfriend and didn't realize that gave Don the opportunity to get his foot inside of the DeLuca house."

On March 28, 1974, Don called over to the DeLuca house and asked to speak with Maria. This time, unlike the others, she decided to take the call. He told her he wanted to take her to prom. Maria was nervous and told him that he would have to meet her Dad first. She explained to Don that if her parents approved of him, she would go to prom with him. He showed up at the house about six o'clock, and didn't leave until well after midnight. He spent almost the entire night talking with Mr. DeLuca about high school wrestling. Don was a superstar at West Tech and Peter was at John Marshall, so they had a lot of mutual interests to speak about.

Even though he was still technically dating Camille, he would call Maria every single day. Maria felt a little funny talking with him, seeing as how he was dating one of her best friends, but she kept giving it a chance. Don saw something he liked; not only a beautiful girl, but also a stable family to live in, which he craved.

On May 3, 1974, Don once again showed up on the DeLuca front steps, this time to bring Maria to church and then meet his mom. It was evening Mass that night that didn't start until 6pm, but he was at the DeLuca home at 4pm. All of her younger brothers and sisters were playing with Don, joking and having fun for the entire two hours before church. As Maria was getting ready, she kept peeking her head out the door and was happy to see how well her family took to him. Maria entered the room wearing a beautiful church dress. Don's face was stunned and happy as he proclaimed he had never dated a girl before who actually wore a dress.

After church, Don took her to meet his mother. Maria could sense he wanted to tell her something important, and he eventually did. He told her that he had broken up with Camille and that he only wanted to date one girl at a time, with that one girl being her. Maria was happy to have a boy genuinely like her, but felt terrible because it ended her friendship with Camile. They didn't speak again for nearly 15 years.

The few weeks of dating Don consisted of him coming over to talk with her father about sports and also to play around with all of her brothers and sisters. It was clear: Don had found a family that he loved being around. They took a lot of walks together and did plenty of talking and getting to know each other on a much deeper level.

The closer they grew together, the greater the fear Maria had of having a seizure in front of him became. At first she could hide the small ones, but she knew she wouldn't be able to hide the big ones. She didn't realize he already knew about her illness and it didn't bug him. She was scared that when he found out he would run away from her like so many others did in the past.

Maria thinks back on the early stages of dating Don, and also the fear of getting sick in front of him: ***"We were at my house most of the time because he liked being around my family so much, so I was protected in case I had one. If I had a small one, I was able to excuse myself from the room and change my underwear and pants if need be. That's the good thing about wearing jeans: you can swap out a pair without anyone noticing.***

I eventually did have one in front of him on a large scale. I remember I was helping change my nephew Tony when I went into a grand mal seizure and blacked out. The next thing I knew, I was waking up in the hospital with Don sitting right next to me. He told me that he knew about my illness all along, and that he didn't care and that he loved me anyway. Eventually they let me go home and Don took me home with my parents as a family. "

Maria saw her doctor a few days after this seizure, and he was irate. He was very upset and he blamed Don. He warned Maria again that she was not allowed to go out with a boy because that would cause seizures. She had not had a Grand Mal seizure in over a year; this was the first big one in a long time, and the doctor was convinced it was Don's fault. He added a new drug to the list she was already taking. It was only two weeks from prom, and sometimes the medicine would take up to a month for Maria to get used to. The doctor would insist that Maria stayed in the hospital until she got used to the new medicine. He was demanding this because he did not want Maria to go to prom or out with any boy ever again.

Maria found a way out of going back to the hospital: ***"I lied and told him if I missed any more school I wouldn't be able to graduate and would also lose my job. I had already missed all the days you could miss, and the teachers were doing their best to work with me after school to help me pass. My dad and I would study hard every night as well to help me pass senior year and graduate."***

The doctor was none too thrilled to hear this, and insisted that she never have these things in life, including a job, a boyfriend or any fun. He insisted that they would only cause seizures. Maria had to beg him that after she graduated and went to prom she would start the new medicine and then go into the hospital. Graduation was only a week away, and Maria lied and told him that she would break up with Don as soon as prom was over.

She had worked so hard to graduate with her senior class by taking summer school courses to get caught up, along with extra study hall hours with teachers. The teachers she had in high school were great and had no issues staying late to help her achieve a dream. They did their best to make her feel good about herself, and she owed it to them as well to finish.

Prom weekend finally arrived, and Maria was never more nervous then she was that day. She had long hair past her shoulders that she played with all day to make sure it was perfect for the big dance. She picked out just the right dress, and it was beautiful. She went to the store with her oldest sister Josephine and spent hours until finding just the right one.

Don showed up early, as usual, 4pm to be exact. All of her siblings were there to keep him entertained while he waited for her. She had been having so many small seizures that day that she didn't get in the dress until the very last moment because she didn't want to risk ruining it. Her sister Josephine fixed her hair, zipped up her dress and told her she looked beautiful. She told her she looked like a princess, with tears rolling from her eyes. Shortly after that, her mother came in and echoed those same sentiments.

As fate would have it, the second her mother and sister walked Maria to the living room so Don could see her for the first time all dressed up beautiful, the damn phone rang and set off a small seizure for Maria. Josephine and her mom quickly hurried Maria into the bathroom and helped her get cleaned up. They put extra padding in her dress and tried everything again. This time she walked out and Don was standing there with the biggest smile on his face. He was holding a full bouquet of flowers and didn't hesitate to let her know how beautiful she looked to him.

Maria reflects on arriving at the prom later that evening: ***"As Don walked me into the ball room at the prom, I felt every single eye on me. Don told me to be strong. I know no one expected me to show up at the prom, and especially with Don McKee, with his notorious reputation. I was the last girl they expected him to be with. The weekend was great, God kept me from having anymore seizures that whole weekend. I felt normal for the first time in my life. It had been so long, I couldn't tell you when the last was I felt that way."***

Another wall put up by her doctor was graduating high school, Maria was not scared of the challenge and worked hard to finish school. The day arrived and, because the John Marshall class of 1974 was so large, the ceremony was held outside in the football stadium. The color scheme had the boys in red caps and the gowns the girls were in white. This helped with the way everyone was seated to spell out the word faith.

Maria was in the "A" section. The word "faith" was very appropriate, because that was what it took to get her there. Maria explains: ***"That's what I held so dear, was faith! As I grew up, no matter what the doctor said I wouldn't do, I had faith in God that I could."***

Receiving a diploma was just one of many obstacles Maria was starting to conquer. She was still working at the nursing home and began to do so full time after high school was complete. A boyfriend, a full time job and a diploma may seem simple to those who take life for granted, but for Maria McKee these were miracles.

Her dream job was to become a beautician one day, but that was still very much out of reach, and rightfully so because she could not stand with a sharp object in her hands with the threat of a seizure always looming. She also had the dream of being a cook for a rich family one day, as well.

With those two dreams still very much far away, she still had time to figure out what she wanted to do following high school. ***"I had to do something, and being a cook for some rich family was only seen on movies and TV at the time. A friend of mine - Gale McEntee - told me about this program they had at TRI-C College for Dental assisting. She helped me sign up for the courses and gave me her books from the class she took. I started the program on Sept 11, 1975."***

Maria went to school during the week at TRI-C and continued to work at the nursing home on weekends. The head instructor, Mrs. Mooney, repeatedly told Maria she was a waste of money and time and did very little to support her passion for achieving anything. She insisted that Maria would never get a job and wasn't smart enough to pass. It didn't help matters that Maria continued to have petite mal seizures that would interrupt the class.

The school bell continued to give Maria issues as well, as the theory portion of the class was held at Jane Adams High School, which was a trade school for girls. The clinic part was held at Case Western Reserve

College in the dental program.

While the course was challenging, it did allow Maria the opportunity to make another close friend. ***"The best part of the 11 month program was meeting a new friend named Anita Rielly. After talking with her I found out my dad was her mailman. She came from a wonderful family. When she found out that I had to take the bus, the rapid, then another bus to get from school to work she offered to start driving me."***

One day, during class, Maria had a grand mal seizure. As she woke up from it, there was Anita sitting next to her, holding her hand and telling her everything would be okay. She knew of Maria's condition because her father had been told about it from Maria's dad. It turned out her family was one of the many praying for Maria throughout her young life without her even knowing it. Anita would continue to be a lifelong friend.

She and Don continued to date past high school, when one day they were walking through Great Northern Mall. Despite the fact that Don only had enough money in his pocket to afford a movie ticket, a cup of coffee and stick of gum, he insisted they walk into the jewelry store. The clerk pulled out a few trays worth of rings and set them in front of the young couple. Until that point in her life, Maria only had two real pieces of jewelry: her class ring and a silver crucifix Sue Hehr gave her for a birthday gift.

Don was enthralled by all the rings on the trays and didn't know which one to choose, so he asked Maria to pick one out. She did - a modest white gold one - and Don asked the clerk how much it cost and how much he would have to put down to reserve it. The clerk said as little as one penny could be put down to reserve it, but you couldn't have it until fully paid for. Don promptly took the rest of the change out of his pocket and reserved the ring.

Later that fall in October of 1975, Don paid for the rest of the ring and made it official. They talked a lot about a future, but didn't make any permanent plans until Don was able to secure a full time job.

Maria continued to take the dental courses at TRI-C, but her seizures continued to worsen as well.

One Friday later that year, Don brought Maria to her doctor's appointment. It was the standard 45 minutes of waiting in the main area, then another 30 minutes of waiting in the exam room. Maria would sit there the entire time, dreading the hands of the doctor about to be all over her.

"He started touching me all over and doing the normal procedure and exam while asking me several questions. It was his typical routine until I grabbed his hand and told him to stop. It was at this point he noticed my engagement ring. I quickly made him aware that I was engaged to be married. He became upset because he did not believe I deserved to be married or happy with anyone. I informed him that Don was in the next room and wanted to meet him.

Don wanted to have a better understanding of what epilepsy was and how he could learn how to better help me cope with it. Don had no idea what epilepsy was other than what he saw me go through and wanted to learn more. The doctor refused to meet him, and told me he never would meet him until I got married, although he reiterated that I never would.

I explained to him that the seizures had been increasing - at least 20 small ones a day - and the Grand Mals were increasing in frequency as well. He proceeded to tell me it was my own fault for going to school, having a job and being in a relationship. He claimed these things were causing it. He honestly believed that if I quit work, quit school and left Don, the seizures would stop. He wanted me to sit in a chair or bed 24 hours a day. His other solution, as usual, was to once again up my medication. The medicine made me very sleepy and had only a small affect on stopping seizures."

One of the side effects from the medicine besides constantly being tired was gaining weight. Maria, who was very small - only weighing about 95 pounds soaking wet with a brick in her hand -ballooned up to a size 7. Then, as she continued to take the medicine, the weight kept piling up until she ballooned to a size 16. She was never that heavy before, and it just added to the ridicule from the teacher at dental school. She insisted that someone as heavy as Maria was becoming would never get a job, let alone with her illness. Maria was done hearing her nonsense, and snapped back at the cryptic teacher by informing her she would prove her wrong like so many others over the course of her life.

On March 28, 1976, Don landed a great job working at RTA as a bus driver. The job was steady employment and even came with health benefits. With the job in place and Maria finishing up dental school, the wedding preparations began. The wedding date was set for November 19, 1976, and Maria was set to finish up dental school in May of 1976. Things were lining up well and looking good.

Maria passed the state board for her dental assistance license and graduated dental school with flying colors. With so many positive things going on, it was almost a shame that she had to go back to the doctor's office, but epilepsy doesn't take a day off for anyone. When she went in for her two month checkup on the new medicine, the doctor was quick to crush every good vibe she had going. He was irate that she was still planning on getting married and had passed her state boards.

Making matters worse was the fact that when her blood work came back it revealed that the toxin levels in her blood were rising because of the new medicine she had been on. The medicine had been working well at stopping seizures, but it was unhealthy for her liver, and she was taken off of it immediately. This caused the Grand Mal seizures to begin once again, and the daily horror to return with them.

Despite Grand Mal seizures returning, Maria's love she shared with Don was true and would not be broken. November 19, 1976 arrived, one day after Don's 23rd birthday. Their wedding day was beautiful and a dream come true. The wedding was held at St. Patrick's in West Park Cleveland. Here was this woman, that thought she would never find love, let alone get married and have children, and now Don was doing everything he could to make those dreams happen for her and with her.

Don really took a chance, and he wouldn't have done so if he wasn't truly in love. It was a fairytale story many thought they'd never see. Maria's story already gave hope to many with epilepsy -having the husband, the job - but she wasn't even close to being done yet.

Don and Maria didn't wait long to try to start a family because they both wanted to be parents badly; plus, when you have Epilepsy you can never count on tomorrow. Each day is a gift because with such a serious condition, you never know how ravaged your body might become. Maria and Don knew the window to start a family would not be open long, and that many would frown upon it because of Maria's condition. That did not stop them, and they kept trying.

Maria reflects back on this exciting and stressful time in her life: ***"We wanted to get our lives started together right away and have a family. All my life I was told I would never be a mommy, and it was so painful to hear those words. Month after month we tried getting pregnant, and month after month we failed, but I was not about to give up. We tried for nine months before I finally missed my period in August of 1977. I received my period very regularly, so this was a slight chance of hope when it didn't arrive.***

The week before I missed my period was filled with Gran Mal seizures, even more so than usual. When they finally stopped for 24 hours, I scheduled a doctor's appointment to get everything checked, including the missed period. I was told it would be two weeks before they could get me in, so I would have to wait."

The two weeks felt like an eternity for Don and Maria to have to wait, but they did. It was a good sign when they eventually got the clearance to bring her urine sample to the doctors, because it was August 16, which is the same week of the Assumption of the Blessed Mother into Heaven. They were told the lab would run tests and they would have word that day by telephone by 4pm with an answer on pregnancy. The minutes turned to hours until the phone finally rang at 5pm, an hour late.

When the call came in, the bells set off a small seizure for Maria. As Don calmed her down and held her, he managed to answer the phone. Don asked the nurse for the results but the nurse refused, saying that she could only talk to Maria about it. The nurse informed Maria that the test came back pregnant. Maria instantly started celebrating by jumping up and down and screaming in joy. Don took the phone and finished the conversation.

Maria and Don went straight to the DeLuca home to share with them the wonderful news. Maria had not told them she was late because she didn't want to worry anyone or get their hopes up. Before Maria and Don could even get the words out, Mrs. DeLuca knew exactly what was going on. She had been pregnant eight times - her oldest daughter Josephine had been pregnant three times - she knew just by looking at Maria's face that she was pregnant.

Everyone was excited! Joe and Rosemarie DeLuca had been told countless times that their daughter could never get pregnant. Her doctor had never hesitated to remind them that Maria shouldn't even try to have kids because it would kill her. Maria wanted children so badly she would even jokingly tell them that she wanted to have nine so she could beat them by one. Joe and Rosemarie believed in their daughter and never let her believe she couldn't do it. They always told her to leave it in God's hands.

So excited with the news of being parents, Don and Maria went straight from the DeLuca home to the maternity store. When the sales girl came up to them, Maria couldn't resist telling her she was pregnant. She had lost all the weight from the previous medicine and was now back down to a size 3. She was so skinny that she didn't need the maternity clothes yet, but the excitement was still very much there. Maria was excited to be like her own mother that she didn't care that the clothes wouldn't fit for months and still bought a bunch of them.

"We went home and I quickly started trying everything on," says Maria. "***I would try on a pair of pants and stuff a pillow under my shirt to make it look like I was several months pregnant. Don would laugh then come give me a hug. Don was as excited as I was, but we both knew we had to start getting serious and look for a new home. We had been living in a tiny one bedroom apartment and knew that was too small to raise a child.***

We eventually found and bought a house on Midvale, just two streets over from my parents on Forestwood in West Park Cleveland. It was important to live near them because I couldn't drive. My sister Josephine was pregnant with her third child with her husband Butch, and her family lived on the street behind my parents called Maplewood. So it was great to be so close to family in case we needed them."

Because she was now pregnant, Maria started to see a female doctor for the first time. This was a big change from her normal doctor appointments, as she explains here: ***"It was the last week in August 1977 when I went for my first OBGYN appointment. I had never seen a female doctor before, and I was very nervous but also excited at the same time. I filled out the paperwork and answered as many questions as I could. When the doctor walked in the only thing I remember is her saying hello and that she was also my sister's doctor. That is when I went into a full blown Grand Mal seizure. "***

Don and Mrs. DeLuca were sitting outside in the waiting room and had no idea what was going on. That is when they saw the nurses and ladies in the billing part of the office jump up and rush into the exam rooms. This was a clue for them that something was seriously wrong. It was a scary moment that led to Maria having to be taken directly to the hospital to be examined.

When her doctor arrived at the hospital to check on Maria, his firsts words were not of comfort, but of disdain. He quickly reminded her that he told her not to get pregnant. Maria corrected him and said he told her she couldn't get pregnant. It was another aggravating moment between doctor and patient. It was at this moment of great stress and drama that everything turned a direction no one saw coming.

The doctor turned to Maria and Don; this was the first time he ever met Don and would turn out to be the last. He told Don that it was his fault that Maria was having seizures and he should have never married her. He insisted that this baby would kill Maria, and it was Don's fault. He then said that because she was only a month pregnant, it wasn't too late for her to abort the baby and that he had already set up the appointment to have it done. He said that he would have no issues killing the baby, and we could tell everyone she had a miscarriage.

Don turned to Maria and told her to get dressed, because they were leaving right now. Maria was so scared that this life already growing inside of her was going to end. Don was pissed off, and rightly so. He told the doctor that Maria would never see him again and he was never to put his hands on his wife ever again, either. Maria was shocked, Don didn't knock him out cold right there. He grabbed her hand, held Maria tight, and they left, never to return to see that doctor again.

As they were leaving the office, the doctor began yelling and screaming and making threats. He said that he was in charge and would call the shots. Maria was on heavy meds at this point, roughly 1200 milligrams a day of Dilatin & 650 milligrams of Phenobarb. She was also on 800 milligrams of Myclian. It was some very heavy dosages that would turn most people into zombies.

After doing research on the drug Myclian, Maria found out that the side effects on pregnant women would be horrible for the child. The baby could be born with a cleft palate, missing limb and a heart murmur. The OBGYN was able to lower the dosages of the drugs for her pregnancy. She also decided to start seeing a new neurologist - Dr. Sanders - and never again returned to Dr. Stone.

Because of her condition, she saw Dr. Sanders every three weeks during her pregnancy. The original due date was May 13, 1978. During the pregnancy, her seizures were never under control but, because of her large family she was never left alone. She stopped working as well, because it was a very high risk pregnancy. Her mother would pick her up every day, attend mass in the morning and spend the rest of the day at her parents' house until Don came home from work. Her family was there to help her every step of the way.

It was March 15, 1978, Maria had only gained 12 pounds and was only 7 months into her pregnancy when once again God had a plan. Maria had a taste for hot Italian sausage that day and began to cook in the kitchen. It was during the time the sausage took to boil in the water that Maria tried to make the most of her time and straighten up around her house. This was one of the few days she was left alone at home. Her parents were gone at a funeral about an hour away; Maria was not up for the trip.

Maria goes on to explain what happened next: ***"I started to straighten up around the house while the sausage cooked on the stove. It felt so good to be able to do things in my own home. I was only 7 months pregnant, and it was much too early to have a baby. I started feeling a pain in my right side. I figured it was just because I was doing a lot of physical things I hadn't done in awhile. My parents were about an hour away and Don was on the road driving the RTA bus. It was very quiet in the house until the buzzer from the dryer went off and sent me into a full blown seizure.***

I felt my entire body collapse as my eyes rolled back in my head and the nightmare began. I clutched my stomach, holding my baby as the nightmare unfolded. I clung to my stomach and gasped for air. I asked God to help the seizure stop because I was so afraid it was going to cause me to lose my baby. I lost control of my bladder, and was laying on the ground in a pool of my own urine until Don came

home around 7pm that evening.

When he got home, I was still in a lot of pain, as it had gotten worse throughout the day. I was scared and so was Don, as I was still only 7 months into the pregnancy. Don called the hospital and they told him to bring me in right away. After a few tests, it was already after midnight and March 16, 1978 had arrived. They broke my water and placed an internal monitor to the baby's head and it picked up no heartbeat, no motion and no movement of any kind. The doctors knew they couldn't wait any longer and it was time for an emergency C-Section, because the baby may be dead."

The DeLucas arrived at the hospital just before Maria went into surgery. Shortly after Maria was wheeled into surgery, they gave her a spinal epidural so she couldn't feel anything. A few minutes later a little boy was born. Donald Joseph McKee was born; he was tiny, as expected for a two-month premature baby to be. He was five pounds at birth. The delivery team didn't hesitate to put oxygen on him to keep him breathing because he was not showing many signs of life. He didn't even cry like most babies do when born.

About an hour later, Maria got to hold her son for the first time. She takes us through this incredible moment: ***"He was all there: ten toes, ten fingers, no cleft palate, just beautiful. My son Donald was absolutely the most beautiful baby in the world. I gave life to this little person. It was a day many never let me believe I could have. "***

They had to put Donald in the NICU because he was starting to tremble and shake. He had all the medicines Maria was on in his system. He went from five pounds down to four in his first 24 hours of being alive. The doctors said he was going through withdrawals from the drugs Maria was on to help treat her epilepsy. It was a week before Maria would be cleared to leave the hospital; her newborn son, however, was not healthy enough. It was a hard period for Don and Maria, as daily they would have to look at the nursery in their home and just wonder and dream as to when they could bring their baby home. It would be five weeks before Donald was healthy enough to come home.

It was a dream come true for Maria and Don, a day many believed would never come for them. They were now parents, and it was everything that they hoped it would be. As nice as it was to be a mother, it didn't make the seizures stop, and they continued to arrive on a regular basis, which limited many of things Maria could do with her baby.

Once again, her family was all around her to help support and raise the child when Don was on the road with RTA. By the blessings of God, Maria never had a seizure while holding the baby. She was surrounded by family at all times. ***"No matter where I went, there was always a sister or brother with me to help. It didn't matter if it was the kitchen or bathroom; someone was with me and the baby. I never had to fear being alone. Even my nephew Tony and niece Gena were there to help with me, as well. They were all wonderful and never made me feel like I was a burden."***

It was a miracle that having the first child didn't kill her. But Maria and Don loved being parents so much they wanted to try for one more. Maria felt that if God didn't want her to have another, then he wouldn't have planted a second seed into her life. Getting pregnant again would be very risky, as the chance of mortality rose. There was a strong chance that she could get through the entire surgery but not make it through delivery. If this occurred, she would leave behind two children and a husband.

The other factor was that even if she got pregnant again, what would be the quality of life she could live? As a little boy growing up in the very early stages of his life, Donald had to watch his mommy seizure right in front of him. Over and over again as a two year, three year and four year old, little Donald would have to witness the scary sadness as his mother convulsed on the ground and his eyes welled up with tears. No little boy should ever have to witness such a sad sight.

Maria reflects back on her son having to witness such horrible things: ***"As Donald grew up, he was wonderful to watch as a little boy. He was so sweet and kind and always watched over me in his own little way. There were too many times he had to watch his mommy go down into a Grand mal seizure. It was so hard to watch him cry over me and hear him scream 'Mommy, Mommy please don't die.' As I would come out of the seizures he would be holding my hand telling me he loved me. Other times it was tough because Don or one of my parents or siblings would have to peel him off of me in tears and lay him in his bed until he cried himself to sleep as I tried to recover myself.***

Depending on the size or length of the seizure, I could be in the hospital for weeks at a time, away from my son. Back then, they wouldn't let children in that part of the hospital. I wasn't there to teach him how to count, how to tie his shoes or how to sing the alphabet. Even if my physical body was there, my brain and limbs were in limbo because of the seizures and medicine."

Despite the constant seizures, the constant pain and everything telling her that it would never happen again, Maria still tried to have another baby for the next several years as the agony continued. She and Don had created life once, and they were determined to give Donald a sibling.

Eventually the trying and praying would pay off, as Maria explains here: ***"It was May 3, 1981, and my husband Don was working in the yard with my Dad and brothers. My sisters Anna and Franny were in the house watching me and Donald. I had missed my period for a week, and my mom brought over this new invention called a home pregnancy test. You would have to pee on the stick and check it later to see if it turned pink or blue, pink meaning pregnant and blue meaning not pregnant. It took three hours for it to work, and those three hours felt like three days. We all just kept waiting and waiting for it to work and give us a sign one way or the other. The stick began to turn pink and my sisters were ecstatic. They kept running in and***

out of the bathroom to look at it.

As we waited, my other two sisters Rose and Josephine showed up to the house to join in on the watch party as well. Before long, all three hours were up and the test was final. Perhaps May 3rd was a good sign, because it was the date of Don and I's first date, as well as the original due date for Donald to be born. It was lucky that day, too, as the test was positive and I was pregnant again.

We hadn't clued in Don or my brothers and Dad as to what was going on, so when they all came back in the house to eat the dinner we made them my mom pulled Don aside because she wanted to give him the good news. At first, he was confused and wondered who took me to the doctors, because the doctors are closed on Saturdays. Josephine then stepped in and explained to him how the home pregnancy tests work. She also made sure to let him know that we still needed to get in with an actual doctor ASAP to know for sure. "

The following Monday, Maria's mom picked her up early; they went to church then straight to the doctor's office. It was nerve racking but worth it, as the nurse said they would have to analyze her urine and call her by 4pm that day with the results; so it would be another day of waiting around for the answer. Mrs. DeLuca explained that the phone ringing could cause issues for Maria, so she asked if they could call the office after four for the results, and the nurse understood and agreed. A little later that day they received the confirmed good news and the celebration began.

"This time my first visit with the OBGYN was not as scary for me. I knew what was going to happen. The only thing that was scary was that I was forced to use a new doctor. It was comforting, however, when the new doctor told me he had researched my history and was aware of all issues. They did not have ultra sounds, however, so we couldn't see the baby grow.

I was on all the same medicine I was on when I was pregnant with

Donald, plus four others to make it 12 different kinds of medicine total. I was consuming up to 80 pills a day. I was still having seizures both big and small despite all the medicine. I was concerned that the medicine would have side effects on my baby like it did with Donald so, on my own without telling anyone, I stopped taking them. The only ones I kept taking were Dilatin and Phenobarb. I had been on those the whole time and didn't want to stop. The other ten I just slowly lessened until I stopped taking them all together. I didn't want to take any chances at hurting the baby. It didn't cause me to stop having seizures, and it didn't increase them either, so it really didn't matter."

Unlike with Donald, this time around Maria gained a lot of weight. She gained 15 pounds in the first two months. By the fourth month, she had gained 26 pounds. By month five, the baby was very active and on October 2, 1981, Maria woke up to constant baby movement in her stomach. This was a big change of pace because with Donald she never even felt a flutter. This baby felt as if it was doing somersaults and back flips in the womb.

The baby movement was constant throughout the day and didn't let up. The constant moving caused spotted bleeding, which is not good for a pregnant woman but common at times, as well. Don was at work and her sister Fran was watching over her and Donald. Fran eventually called the doctor, as Maria began to experience extreme pain. Fran dropped Donald off at the neighbors and then called for an ambulance.

When the ambulance arrived, Fran sat up front with the drivers and the paramedics in the back worked on Maria. Fran begged them not to blare the sirens in fear it would cause a seizure, which was the last thing Maria needed to go with the intense pain in her stomach. The news they received when they got to the hospital was not what they had expected: the baby had kicked out Maria's appendix, and it was about to burst. The pain was unreal and Maria, not understanding what was going on, was worried that all the pain and craziness meant she was losing her baby. All the pain and anxiety was also causing her to have constant seizures.

The doctors needed to get the appendix removed right away before it killed her. Eventually Maria's parents entered the room to help calm Maria down. They had a priest with them from St. Pat's named Father Bob Linquist. He came to the hospital to give Maria an anointing of the sick prayer. Meanwhile, Don's car had broken down and he was walking back home, completely unaware of what was even going on.

As they were rolling her into the operating room, they explained to Maria that this type of procedure typically only takes about an hour. Because of all the complications with the epilepsy and seizures, they could only give her a heavy dosage of Novocain and not put her to sleep during it. They also gave her a very small sedative as they started to cut.

It was an intense experience that Maria made it through. When she woke up the next day, she was in the hospital bed next to Don, and he had a rosary in his hand. Marias recalls: ***"My first words to him were asking if the baby was still alive inside me. His eyes were blood shot from crying and no sleep. I was relieved when he told me the baby was okay and I was still pregnant."***

The stress and worrying of what was starting to happen inside of her body caused Maria to then lose 19 of the 25 pounds she had gained. It didn't affect the baby, however, as it was as still active as ever with a strong heartbeat.

The next three months flew by, and on January 13, 1982, Maria was over at her parents for the day, as was the usual case when Don was at work. The baby was moving extra hard that day, almost as if it was doing jumping jacks. The constant activity inside of her also made it feel as if the incision, still fresh from her surgery, may split open. Her incision from the appendectomy was 18 inches in length and half way around the right side of her body. It looked like a perfect C. When Don arrived to pick her and Donald up, he could sense Maria was in too much pain once again, and left Donald at her parents and brought Maria to the hospital.

Maria walks us through that chaotic day: ***"My mom had already called the doctor's office and was waiting for the call back from them. She screamed on the phone, 'She is going to have this baby. I have had eight babies and I know when one is coming, how many have you had?' She then turned to Don and told him we needed to get to the hospital.***

I was only in my first week of my eighth month and the baby was still small. The seizures were also coming one after another. They were petites and not grand mal, but when you have enough they really start to hurt."

There were a lot of questions and concerns about having a C-Section surgery to deliver the baby because Maria was fresh off another major surgery just months prior. There was no other way to have the baby, however, and they would have to find a way to make it work. Luckily that day the chief of staff for doctors was on duty, and was able to step in and perform the C- Section. Within an hour of giving Maria the spinal, the doctor delivered a five pound 2 ounce baby boy. The baby was named Vincenzo Peter McKee, after his great grandfather on his mother's side. When Don phoned back to the DeLuca house with the news, Donald was so ecstatic that he started jumping up and down on the bed screaming, ***"I have a baby brother, I have a baby brother!"***

The baby would spend two days in the NICU because of the possibility of medicine withdraws, such as Donald went through. There was only a small trace of Dilantin in his system, so the hospital stay wasn't long this time, and within a week they were all home as a family. The doctors were impressed at his ability to respond to movement in the room, and even mentioned how he would be really good with words - one day, perhaps, a world famous author if the breaks fell right. The kid just looked like a genius!

Maria knew the sacrifice to get pregnant again would be huge, and sure enough it was. The next 16 months were hell for her. She started having three Grand Mal seizures a day, the most in her life, and the petites were constant in between. There were constant trips in and out of the hospital and also constant drug switches, trying to get things back in order and figured out. The constant seizures left her a vegetable most of the time, having to sit on pads so she wouldn't hurt herself too bad with the seizures. She wasn't able to take care of her new baby, Vince, and things just kept getting worse.

Making things worse was that Vince started walking at eight months old and was running all over the house all the time. He was so intelligent and active that nothing could contain him. She wasn't able to chase him, so Donald had to follow him everywhere in the house like a shadow. ***"I'd try to spend as much time with the boys as possible, but never alone because you never knew when I would go into another Grand mal seizure. The meds increased and 90% of the time I didn't even know what day it was. If it wasn't for my husband being such an angel, I never would have made it though those times. Vince and Donald ended up living with my parents most of the time, as I was constantly in this vegetable state and in the hospital. I never got to play with them, and when I was home I was so drugged up I didn't even know my own name,"*** Maria said.

Donald would never leave his mother's side when home; however, Vince didn't even realize he had a mommy at his very young age. She was never around, and he didn't know any better. Maria never fed him, never changed his diaper, never got to do the normal mommy-son things you do with a baby in the first two years of their life. To baby Vince, Maria was nothing more than a face laying in a bed or sitting motionless in a chair.

Then one day there was a knock on the McKee door, it was a new mailman. His name was Mike Perna, and he and Joe DeLuca started together in the post office many years prior. Mike told Maria that he had a doctor that could possibly help her. He was also epileptic and had been for the last 29 years. Maria takes us through that day, of meeting Mike and hearing his story that would eventually help her: ***"It was right in the midst of the worst time in my life. This man comes in my house, explains who he is and picks up the phone to call his doctor for me. He even made the appointment for me with his doctor. The appointment was set for March 28, 1983. I was positive that something good was going to happen, and the chance was strong that my life may be changed forever."***

Maria arrived at 6pm on March 28, 1983, in Dr. Victor Victoroff's office alongside of her parents and husband. Dr. Victoroff was a tall man, with straight white hair and thick black glasses. The good doctor asked questions to everyone in the room for nearly a half hour straight as he examined Maria. He was amazed that after the first 27 years of her life, with everything she went through, that she was even able to walk. He explained that the only thing he thought they should do to make the seizures stop was brain surgery. He stated that all the medicine in the world was not going to help. They had tried everything, and brain surgery was the last option.

Dr. Victoroff went on to explain that there was a hospital in Montreal, Canada called the Montreal Neurological Institute that was partnered with the McGill University, and they were the only ones able to do the very risky and controversial surgery. It was the top medical college in the world. Some of its graduates had won the Nobel Peace Prize for producing some of the top equipment in the medical fields in the world, and their top priority was finding a cure for brain disease. It also had a good history of successful brain surgeries, as the first ever successful one was done there.

Maria was not bothered by the distance needed to travel for the miracle surgery. After 27 years of pure hell, any distance was worth traveling for a shot at a miracle. ***"I told him to make all the arrangements because***

nothing was going to keep me from going. I would have walked there if that's what it took. I never asked him how much the surgery would cost because we already owed thousands upon thousands of dollars in medical bills, so at this point it was like adding a mole hill to a mountain."

Dr. Victoroff informed Maria, Don and the DeLucas they would be receiving a letter from the Montreal Neurological Institute with all the pertinent information regarding the surgery. The concern was great, as brain surgery at that time was still pretty much unheard of and the risks were heavy. The casualty rate was high of people dying during the surgery and slightly afterwards.

As time went on, Maria waited each day for that letter to show up, much like a child waits for Christmas. She wasn't given a time table for when they could have the surgery preformed, so it could be years. ***"I was so excited I waited for the mail everyday as Mike came to the door. He would check on me if I was home. He knew what I was waiting for. One day I was at my parents' house and my Dad came home with the letter. Mike had given it to him to personally deliver to me because Mike knew I wasn't home that day, but at my parents."***

The words inside of the letter read:

"***Dear Maria McKee,***

I have received all the medical history on you and would like to examine you at M.N.I for one or two months to see if you qualify for surgery."

Maria was disappointed at the words "qualify for surgery," as she was thinking it was more of a definite conclusion that she was getting one and the letter was supposed to say that instead. ***"I was all ready to go at a moment's notice. The letter explained I needed to be there on May 24, 1983. It was only the second week of April, so I knew there was still a little bit of time to wait. Don made all the arrangements***

at work to use his vacation time so he could to drive me up there and be with me. We didn't even have enough money to fly, so we knew we were in a for a long road trip.

We had a 13 hour ride to Quebec. My brother Pete had given me a special going away gift. It was a clown called Jude. He gave it to me to entertain the children and lighten the mood. Jude is also a religious name, as St. Jude is the patron Saint of hopeless causes. We stayed at my parents' house the night before so we could be close to the boys."

The alarm went off early and the car was packed and ready to go. The kisses goodbye came with a lot of tears. Maria loved them all, each member of her family, but the fear was there that she may be seeing them for the final time. Little Donald clung to his mother for dear life. He had been though more sadness as a five year old then most people have to go through their entire life. She then said goodbye to her little baby Vince. At 16 months he had been sparred knowing what was really going on. He didn't seem to realize that Maria was even his mother, but just a woman he continued to see at times - he was more concerned with finishing his Rubik's cube toy he had been given. At 16 months old, he could put it together quicker than most 5 year olds.

Unlike most road trips where cars are packed with excited families eager to reach a fun destination, this one was crammed with four people all trying not to think about the worst. Maria knew she needed to remain strong and not let her family know how scared she was. ***"I was never so scared in my life. Staying strong was one of the hardest things I ever had to do. My dad had the whole trip planned down to the minute, even the rest stops. The trip was filled with prayers and stories. My mom packed food and snacks so we all ate while we drove. It was at one of the rest stops, however, that a near tragedy happened. We were in Syracuse, New York and while getting out the car, I wasn't quick enough with my hands, and my dad accidentally smashed it in the door real hard. Four of my fingers were broken and there was***

blood everywhere."

Normally in a situation like this, a person would be rushed to the hospital, but Maria refused to go to a hospital when she was already on her way to a hospital. Don and her father taped it up with gauze and bought a bunch of popsicles for her to hold for the rest of the trip. It was insane, but at this point, she had come so far, nothing was going to stop her from completing the trip.

At around six in the evening, they eventually arrived in Montreal. Maria's hand was throbbing in pain still, but she was happy to arrive. They were eager to get some rest, as the tests were set to start the next day. Rest would not be easy, as there was a high school prom going on in the same hotel and the music was blaring all night long. All four of them were in the same room, and eventually Joe DeLuca had enough, getting up to scold the youngsters for being too loud.

May 24 arrived, and the hotel was still about an hour away from the hospital. They wanted to stop at a church and thank God for getting them this chance. They stopped at the Saint Joseph Oritory, a small church inside of a big Cathedral covered in crutches, wheelchairs and canes. This place was a place where thousands were healed. It was a perfect place to pray before entering the hospital. They couldn't stay long because they needed to get to the hospital and, not knowing exactly where they were, they didn't want to take any chances at getting lost, mixed in with the factor that more than 90% of the people there spoke French.

They would eventually arrive at the hospital, which was very big and very clean. It was also very old. It was quiet as well, with wide hallways, but not very much hustle and bustle. The nurse showed Maria her room in the ward. It almost appeared to be the docks at a military camp. Each ward had two rows of beds, ten each lined up with small foot lockers at the bed of each one. There was a small night table next to each bed, as well.

An hour later, Maria was saying goodbye to her parents, as they had to drive back and leave her. It was brutal for the DeLucas to leave her behind, but the institute didn't allow them to stay. The nurses began doing all the normal things you do when being checked in to the hospital. They showed Maria where she would get her meals and laundry done during the stay. It was very different. They also kept their patients in color-coordinated wristbands. Each color on the wristband was for something different. It determined food, meds, allergy and illness, along with vital information such as name and date of birth.

It was very different because, as a patient, you went to the hospital café for your meals and you had to wash your own clothes and dress up in formal wear every morning unless there was a test scheduled to take first thing in the morning, then you could stay in your gown. The diversity of the patients was also great: in Maria's ward alone - a room filled with 20 patients - only three of them were actually from Canada - the rest had come from all over the world.

Maria explains some of her early memories from the institute: ***"I remember sitting right across from me was this elderly woman in a wheel chair who resembled my dead grandmother. Her name was Natalie DeLuca. What were the odds that we would have the same last name? Of course she was Italian. She was 80 years old and told me not to worry because she and the other patients would be my family while I was in there."***

Every test they did they explained what they were doing by performing it on another patient first so the patient could better understand the reasoning behind it. This allowed the patient to ask plenty of questions, as well. For the first two weeks all the tests were done, which allowed Maria still to be able to walk to the area of the huge hospital to have them done. Other times, the testing would be done at McGill University and the patients would be driven over. The testing was incredibly unique, using everything from ink blot tests to card games to study how her brain worked. The doctors, students and nurses would write down and study her every move.

One day for twelve straight hours, they sat Maria down and stuffed all kinds of different medical cotton swabs in her nose, asking her what she smelled. There was no right or wrong answers, but each one helped. It was showing them how her brain worked and what reactions it would cause. Some smells were beautiful, and others would cause her to vomit - she never knew what was coming next.

There was also the picture test. This consisted of hanging a picture in front of Maria, one at a time, some clear some fuzzy. Some had solid colors and some had many different wild colors. One test involved numbers with basic addition, subtraction and division problems for the patient to figure out. Each day was filled with a different test, almost like high school with each subject being tested. There was even a test in a small gym where they had Maria run laps, jump rope and other various physical testing. The testing helped the doctors examine Maria, but also caused seizures.

Another reason for the testing was to chart tendencies and see if anything would change after the possible surgery. They would put the patient through all the same testing after the surgery to see if the answers were different and also look for drastic improvement in certain areas.

Maria was moved into a private room starting the third week of her stay. Starting that day, they hooked her up to a machine called Telemetry. They inserted close to a hundred fine wires into her head. They also injected wire through her jaw bones and throughout her entire body. She was then hooked up to a robot-looking machine, which caught her every move on video tape. She was more or less confined to a bed the entire week. They didn't even want her getting up to use the bathroom, instead having her pee in the catheter and use a bed pan for bowel movements.

During this week they brought in all of her meals, and she was forced to watch a lot of television and lay in bed. They also gave her plenty of books to read during that third week, as well. Other patients that she had become friends with would come in to visit. No one who was there was for just a night, as everyone was there at least a month, which allowed everyone to get close with each other.

It was also during that week that Maria finally met her doctor. Dr. William Fiendel was the Chief of Staff and the Dean of the McGill University. He was of medium height with blue eyes, white hair, slightly balding and a calm demeanor. Dr. Fiendel explained to Maria that he was the man - with God's help - who would stop the horrible seizures. He also explained to Maria the reason for all the testing she had been going through. He and his team of doctors had been studying the results of each test so he could completely understand exactly how Maria's brain worked. By doing this, it would also help him determine if Maria even needed the surgery or just a different medical regiment. He explained to Maria that it would still be awhile before he made his final decision, and many tests still had to occur.

They had taken Maria off her medicine while there as well, so they could see her brain in a natural element. This caused her seizures to be out of control and constant. They were getting stronger and larger each time. While she was having her's at times, she would look over and other patients were having them, as well. It was the first time she had to witness someone else go through the hell that had plagued her life. For the first time, she saw how horrible they were to have to watch. All she could think of was her poor husband and son, having to watch her go through that so many times.

The third week was the hardest, but once it was over they were unable to unhook her from all those machines and needles jabbed in her. Her arms and legs had been strapped down for an entire week straight, so when they finally unstrapped her the nurses had to help her stand up. It took a while for her body to find its natural state where she could walk and move on her own.

Maria was there three more weeks, and the tests continued along with vials of blood work being done. These tests included another spinal tap, MRIs, cat scans and various other tests. The final big test that would put all the pieces together was called an N.E.O.M.R. which takes place in a coffin-like bed with wires plugged in all over the patient's body. It also required Maria to wear ear plugs with microphones in them. She was then placed in a large box for 12 hours, where she couldn't see anything or move. The machine allowed them to see her internal organ function. The testing was so intense and accurate that the machine knew what Maria was going to do before she did it. They let her know when she was going to move a finger before she did it, they even knew when she was going to urinate before she did it; the machine read everything three steps ahead. The doctors used the headphones to communicate with Maria, and even pray with her at times.

Maria reflects back: ***"I was scared, but at this point in my life I just wanted to be normal, I wanted to be the wife my husband deserved. I wanted to be a mother to my children, and I was willing to go through hell to make it happen. After being there six weeks, we finally got the news we wanted, as I had qualified for the surgery. Dr. Fiendel said that he wasn't sure of the date yet, but in the meantime I needed to go home and be with my family. He said it was important that I see my boys and my parents one last time. He stated it would be an important way to get me mentally prepared for my surgery."***

Don called home and let everyone know the news and what had been decided. Maria would be coming home, but they needed to be prepared because the seizures would be worse. The doctors had stopped Maria from taking any medicine other than baby aspirin to get her ready. Maria returned home on July 8, 1983, and the surgery was set for September 23, 1983.

Donald's very first day of school in the first grade was September 12,

1983. Maria was not there, as she was on her way back to Canada that same day; yet another important event Maria had to miss because of her terrible illness. On one of the most important days of a child's life, he had to start it without his mother. Epilepsy had reared its ugly head once again, tearing a family apart at every chance.

Father Bob Linquist had come through with an airplane ticket for Maria to fly to Montreal. He would also provide one for Don the week of the surgery. The night before Maria's flight, Father Bob held a special mass at St. Patrick's Church for Maria. The church had well over 1,000 people in attendance that evening, all praying hard for Maria, some of which didn't even know Maria personally, but knew of the cause and believed strongly in finding a way to make sure she was healed.

Maria reflects back on that emotional night: ***"I could feel the power of God's presence around me that evening. It was an electrifying feeling but, at the same time, it helped me feel very much at peace with what was about to happen. As everyone left the church, they came up to me and hugged me. Everyone wanted to hold my hand or touch my shoulder, wishing me good luck. It was the first time I had that feeling of support outside of my family. It is a memory I will never forget."***

The week before the surgery Maria had the chance to sit in on the surgery of another brain patient. It was their policy to let a patient watch the surgery and see everything that went on during one before they had their own. Maria noticed that the patient had a mirror on the wall above the surgery table with pictures of his wife and children on it. She was told that as long as something was sterilized, it could be in the operating room with the patient for comfort. They told Maria she could bring in almost anything she wanted to help her get through it when the time for her surgery came, with the exception of having her husband in the room.

"My mind started to think of what I wanted that would help get

me through when I had mine. I wanted a picture of Don and my children, also a picture of my brothers, sisters and parents, as well. I would also want to bring the tiny statue of Mary I brought with me for every extended hospital stay. I also had a picture of Jesus with me, surrounded by tiny gold metals. The metals represented various saints and had been given to me throughout my life. As I grew up, people would give me the metals of their favorite saint, and I would keep them on the chain. I also wanted a tiny bottle of Holy Water with me."

As Maria was thinking about all the things she would want with her during surgery, she heard a voice calling her: it was David, the man on the surgery table. He knew she was witnessing the surgery, and Maria didn't hesitate to respond with a good luck and God Bless to her fellow patient.

The doctors began to walk in all around David, and they were each a specialist in their field. Everything from heart doctor to lung doctor to even kidney doctor, all the organs that keep a body functioning. There was a psychologist to the very right of the patient, the same one that was asking all of the questions to them throughout the course of the months of research. He would have all the data with him that he compiled, and knew each patient inside and out. He would also ask questions to the patient to see how they were improving during the actual surgery.

David was fully prepped for surgery, and what Maria witnessed next was chilling to the bone for anyone, even people who wouldn't have to endure, simply seeing it was enough. The first doctor cut the scalp, and David let out a primal scream of agony. David screamed it wasn't as bad as a seizure, but still very bad. The muscles in his head wouldn't be cut, but rather pulled and stretched apart with clamps as the patient's head was stuck in a brace and couldn't move. The doctor then took a drill and began to drill David's skull. The drill went right through the skull bone, and the scream David let out was even more horrifying than the first one. Despite the pain, he couldn't move, because every part of his body was clamped down.

After the latest intrusion from the drill, David passed out from the pain. With him out, the doctors were then able to finish by sawing open the rest of his skull and removing the cap. Maria had to witness this because she was about to go through it herself, a man getting his head drilled open and then scalp sawed open. As this was happening, there was a psychologist with Maria, observing her. She was hooked up to machines monitoring her brain waves and entire system as she watched the horror in front of her eyes.

The sawing and cutting took about two hours before Dr. William Feindel walked into the surgery room and took over for the actual surgery to begin. Dr.William Feindel, O.C., G.O.Q., MDCM was one of Canada's most distinguished neurosurgeons. Inducted in 2003, he was a member of the Canadian Medical Hall of Fame. He held honorary degrees and membership in the Order of Canada, the Ordre national du Québec (Grand Officier), the Académie des Grand Montréalais, and the Royal Society of Canada.

After about five hours into the surgery, Maria was removed from the observatory room and taken back to her room where a nice meal of beef stew and dumplings with Cherry Pie and Pepsi was waiting for her from her hospital family. Maria was tired; she had been up since 6am and had to watch what was going to be done to her in a few days. She was mentally and physically exhausted as the techs came in and unhooked her from the various machines. She wanted to rest, but it simply wasn't in the cards.

It was time for physical therapy, as Maria was wheeled into the gym. She was placed on the treadmill and was told to start walking. She did so, gradually increasing in speed as the machine went. As she was walking the nurse was massaging her legs and keeping everything loose. It put her body in the perfect state for surgery in a few days.

Walking back from therapy, Maria saw one of the nurses in charge of David and asked how the rest of the surgery went. Maria was told he was doing great and in his room, recovering with his wife next to him. They were able to remove all of the brain scarring, and he would finally be able to live a normal life. This news brought great joy to Maria's heart and a certain inner peace to her soul. After witnessing David's surgery, Maria was even more confident and ready to have her own. She was ready to endure a lot of pain, but the idea of never again having a seizure was too much to pass up.

There was only one day left before surgery, and it had been 11 days since Maria returned to Canada. Don was on his way there, and Maria had been missing him terribly. She called her parents' home - the one she grew up in - the house that she had endured so much pain, but also so many good times as well. She was lucky enough that her son Donald hadn't left for school, and she was able to speak to him. Donald asked his mom when she would be coming home, and Maria didn't even know if she would make it out of surgery alive, so she didn't want to make any empty promises to her young son. She simply told him she would be back after the doctors were done fixing her.

Maria reflects back on what could have been one of the final conversations with her son: ***"For the first time, I didn't have an answer for him when he asked when I was coming home. I didn't want to lie to him, either.***

It was hard, because when I asked him about school, the news wasn't good. He didn't like it and said that the teacher was mean to him. My niece Frances was in the same class and confirmed the story. Donald explained that he would cry in class because he missed his mommy, and the teacher was very mean to him about it. It was very hard to hear, and it made me feel useless. I asked God to give my little boy strength, the strength I couldn't because I wasn't there to protect him."

The pre-op day would start at 2pm by having Maria get her bowels cleaned out, and then she had to take a special bath that was intended to clean out her pores. She was only able to wear a special hospital gown. No eating, no drinking anything but water, and she was not allowed to walk around freely. She had to stay stationary in her room until surgery at 6am the following day.

It was only 9 am, so Maria knew she still had about 5 hours left to get a few things done before the lockdown would occur. She went and visited David. It hadn't even been 24 hours since his surgery, but he was sitting up and looking good when Maria walked in. When she asked how he was, he didn't waste any time assuring her it was the right move. He explained how great it felt not to have a seizure. He hadn't had one since he got out of surgery. He assured Maria that she could do it, and with her faith in God she was in a good place heading into it.

After her visit with David, she had a huge lunch in the cafeteria. She knew it would be her last before surgery, and maybe ever. When she returned to her room, a nurse was waiting for her with a gallon of liquid for her to drink to prepare her system for the colonoscopy she was about to endure. Following the enema, it was time for the giant bath. They lowered her into a large metal tank that had jets of water and some ammonia-smelling liquid spray out of it onto her. It was brutal and intense, but the whole ordeal only lasted about 5 minutes before the nurse pulled her out and began cleaning her off, then placed her in the gown.

Upon returning to her room, she noticed that all of her personal belongings were gone. The ones in which she asked to be with her during surgery had already been moved into the operating room. The room was clean with new sheets, and everything was brand new and sterile. She knew Don was on his way and she would get to see him at 6 o'clock. The excitement mixed with anxiety caused her to have a massive grand mal seizure while she was waiting. She hadn't been given any medicine since her return to Canada because it was vital she went into the surgery with nothing but normal toxins in her body. No outside influences would be allowed into her system.

When she was all cleaned up from the seizure and resting comfortably trying to recover, it wasn't too much longer until her next test in toughness and mental fortitude was to occur. A man with a pair of clippers walked into the room - it was haircut time. He lifted a towel off a tray, and sure enough, sitting there was a pair of shiny new electric clippers, primed and ready to shave her head clean. He also had a straight edge razor and shaving cream. Maria didn't care about the hair as much as she did her husband seeing her like this. She asked them to wait until after Don arrived, but they couldn't.

At the time, her hair was very long: all the way past her shoulders and down to the midpoint of her back. The barber put it into pony tail form and cut it. He cut as much as he could, but the hair was so thick it would eventually take the electric razors to finish the job and give Maria her first ever buzz cut. A haircut, an enema, a salt bath: none of it mattered compared to the hell she had been through and the hell still yet to come the next day. As the hair fell all over the floor and on Maria, she began to cry. Not because she was upset to lose her hair - that was a very small price to pay for a new chance at life - but because she wanted Don to see her one more time with hair.

Maria looks back: ***"I didn't want Don to see me like this. The man lathered my head with shaving cream and then pulled out the straight razor to finish the job. I was completely bald, no nubs , no anything. They even shaved off my eyebrows. The man handed me a mirror, and I closed my eyes. When I opened them back up, I could see my brother Pete's face looking back at me. Pete had shaved his head a few times in high school because his football coach asking the team to do so. When I looked in the mirror, I could only see and think about Pete.***

I then began to laugh at all I had been through that day. My

bowels were pretty much empty from the liquid I had to drink. They had to give me another bath to clean me off from everything that was coming out of my body that day. This bath was due to getting all the pieces of shaved hair off of me."

After the latest bath, Maria returned to her room and prepped to be strapped in for the night. She did get under the sheets and propped the bed upright so she could see Don when he walked in. She talks about that emotional moment here: ***"I took a sheet and covered up my head like a veil, to try to hide my baldness. Well, the second Don walked into the room I jumped up in excitement and the veil went flying off, I didn't care! I started to cry as I jumped into his arms. He gave me a kiss, held me and told me that he loved me. He had always been there right with me in the seven plus years of our marriage. Don was my world, the only person outside of my family that I truly felt loved me. That first doctor told me that I would never have that kind of love. I wouldn't accept it, I prayed hard to Jesus and the mother Mary to help me find that love, and sure enough they placed Don in my life. They don't come better than him. "***

Don knew exactly what to do and also what to bring to help Maria be at ease the eve before the most important day of her life. He brought a bunch of pictures from home, along with a cassette tape with all the voices from her family members and children on it talking to her. It was a special message from Donald that really touched her. Her young son reminded her how much he loved her and wanted her to come home. He told her that he would take care of her and how much he missed her. At only 5 years old, it was a lot for Donald to have to go through; his mommy was gone.

When the emotional ride of the rollercoaster was over, Don slid into bed and held his wife, re-assuring her that no matter what happened the next day, everything would be all right and he would always love her. Maria reflects: ***"I wasn't afraid of anything they were going to***

do to me, not even the fact that they were going to cut me open wide awake. But to know that I might die and never feel my husband's arms around me again, I suddenly got scared and didn't want him to leave me. The nurse knocked on the door and Don jumped out of bed. The nurse told him he had to leave because it was already 10pm, and I had to go to sleep. My wake up time was set for 4am and I would need some semblance of sleep. I gave Don a kiss goodbye and he pulled out a lollipop from his pocket and said,'Goodnight Telly.' Telly Savales was an actor who was bald and always had a lollipop in his pocket."

As Maria fell asleep that night, the angels in heaven were working overtime watching over her and preparing her soul for its greatest journey. The name of and destination of that journey was freedom. She had gone her whole life emotionally, physically and mentally crippled from a condition that no human being should ever have to endure. And now, after over a quarter of a century of dealing with hell, she would have her chance to fight against the greatest villain in her life. It was a battle with the greatest prize on the line. Once again, that prize was freedom. Freedom from the prison epilepsy had held her body, mind and soul captive of for so many years prior.

She was over 1,000 miles away from her bed, her sons, her parents and the only place she ever knew as home. She was away from those who supported her, and those of which who didn't throughout her life, as well. Everything was behind her and what awaited her could be glorious if she could get there. But like a wise man once said, sometimes it's hell getting to heaven. Her head was going to be cut open; not only that but it would be with a drill and a saw with no Novocain.

She had a lifetime of seizures, of torment, of pissing herself, doctors, hospitals, embarrassment and never knowing when the next attack would occur. A lifetime of being scared, wondering when the hell would come back, when the pain would ever let up. Not even end, but simply give her a pain-free day. For the first 99 percent of her life, it seemed as though that would never occur. Now, she was in Canada, surrounded by geniuses and about to take the chance of a lifetime. This was it, one more trip to hell for a chance at heaven.

September 23, 1983 had arrived. The nurses came in bright and early and scooped Maria up out of bed. They brought her down to the special bathtub, rinsing her down with the special solution. They dried her off, put the gown back on and brought her back up to the room where Don was waiting for her. He had a gown on over his clothes so he was able to hug her. It was less than an hour until surgery, and Maria was ready.

Dr. Feindel walked into the room and introduced himself to Don. It was the first time they had met. Dr. Feindel explained that if they could not cure the epilepsy with the surgery without causing serious damage to other parts of me, then he wouldn't do it. He told them that he would not take away one illness just to give the patient 9 new ones. He explained that if he was going to remove a piece of her brain with scar tissue on it, that he would only do it if it wasn't a part she needed to see, hear, feel, walk, or any other vital function. He was going in her brain for one reason: to remove tissue and stop seizures. If it wasn't possible, then he would stop the surgery. He was not willing to take risks to make things worse for her.

Maria and Don were in agreement with the doctor. Maria then turned and reached for the holy water. In this jug was holy water from every shrine the blessed Mother Mary had appeared at in Fatima. It was also mixed in with 12 ounces of holy water blessed by Pope John Paul II. Maria informed Dr. Feindel that she needed to bless him with the holy water before she would allow him to perform the surgery on her. Dr. Feindel agreed and bent down so Maria could bless his forehead. She also blessed his hands and feet, as she knew he would be on them up to 12 hours during the operation. She then blessed Don with it, and had him bless her with it as well. Dr. Feindel suggested that the rest of the water come into surgery with them. Not only would the holy water be brought in, but it would be poured on Maria at certain parts of the surgery as she prayed. Dr. Feindel knew that it was key to keep Maria calm during the surgery, and this would help. He was a great man to allow such an intense request.

As the moving bed rolled down the hall to the operating room, and Maria inched closer to the surgery that would hopefully save her life and make it worth living, Don was right by her side holding her hands. David was standing there, along with the other patients, and they were wishing her well. She said goodbye to Don as they wheeled her in and she told him she loved him one last time. The moment of truth had arrived.

The procedure started the same way David's did, with numerous doctors entering the room and getting everything prepped. Maria had her entire body strapped down, unable to move in any way. Her head was positioned inside of small metal cage, and the nurse rubbed a cold cream all over her bald skull to prep it for surgery. The sawing began and Maria was in intense pain, but she knew all the screaming in the world wouldn't make it stop and she also knew this is what needed to happen. The doctors took turns, drilling and cutting for what seemed like hours.

As the intense pain of the drilling was filling Marias body, she tried to focus on the man in front of her who was repeating the Our Father over and over. She just kept repeating Jesus's name as the sickening feeling and sound of the drill split her head wide open. It was the worst pain she had ever felt in her life. They needed to drill three holes total, in the shape of a triangle. Once the first whole was drilled into her skull, they inserted a sharp wire that went under the skull cap and through the other two holes, as well underneath the skull cap so they didn't have to touch the brain.

When all the drilling, stretching and sawing was done, her brain was swollen, but ready for the rest of the surgery to take place. Her brain was totally exposed and she could see it through the mirror on the ceiling. Maria did not freak out from watching it because she had witnessed David just a few days prior. It was at this moment that something truly unique happened; the doctor took her skull cap off the tray and let Maria hold it in her hands. It was as light as a feather. Unfortunely, the drilling wasn't done just yet - they still had to drill 10 more holes in her skull. These would be the holes they would need to use later on to insert and pin the skull cap back on with nickel pins.

The worst part of the surgery was over, and now it was time for Dr. Feindel to take over. They began with what is called "mapping the brain." This is done to see what part of the patient's body was controlled by each part of the brain they would be working with. They would insert a fine wire into the brain, and when they would touch that Neurogen with it a part of the body would react. It didn't take long for the doctors to realize her brain was far from normal. When they touched a nerve that should have caused her to urinate, instead it made her right pinky move. When they touched a part of her brain that should have made her cry, instead it made her wink. It was very clear early into the surgery that they were going to have numerous issues to contend with.

The neuro testing went on for the next six hours, as they were hoping to find the scarred neuron that was causing her to have seizures and attempt to fix it. After they had roughly 366 wires through her entire brain without finding the one scarred neuron causing the seizures, the doctor was ready to throw in the towel. Maria blacked out and a miracle would occur.

When Maria opened up her eyes Dr. Fiendel explained to her that she had gone into a grand mal seizure. Her heart and all functioning organs had stopped, and it appeared she had died on the table. When she came out of the seizure and her body kicked back in, Dr. Feindel was able to find the scar tissue causing the seizures. They would spend the next four hours fixing them. After ten hours, the surgery was close to being done and Dr. Feindel left the operating room as the last doctor would focus on putting Marias skull back together with 12 nickel pins, and sewed the cap back together.

As the doctors and nurses from the surgery retired back to their quarters, a whole new slate of doctors and nurses took things over from there and observed Maria in the recovery room. It was in the recovery room that Dr. Fiendel walked in to check in on her. His first question to Maria was asking her if she knew who he was, and Maria answered correctly. He then asked her what her name and birthday were; she answered both of those correctly, as well.

Dr. Fiendel then brought Don into the room to see his wife after 10 plus hours of waiting and worrying. She spent the next two hours with Don and Dr. Fiendel, talking about the surgery and everything that happened during it. Don gave her a kiss on the hand before the nurses wheeled her back to her room. As she was being rolled down the hallway she saw David. He was standing in his doorway with a big smile on his face, a smile so big it looked like half of the moon.

Her brain was already working properly only hours after the surgery, and Don picked up the phone and called home so his wife could hear the sounds and voices of those she loved. After speaking with her parents, siblings and son Donald, she hung up and began to rest. Don fixed the blankets around her and sat with her until she fell asleep. He had to leave the next day because of the arrangements that were made.

Over the following three weeks, Maria would be put through every test that was given to her before surgery to see how her brain improved. It was vital to see if the tests showed improvement and to make sure nothing got worse. Maria hadn't had any issues: no seizures, no shocks, not even a jolt; she just kept getting stronger each day. By the third day post surgery, she was able to walk on her own, and even go to the library at the school and read. She took great enjoyment in sitting on the balcony of the hospital and looking over to the soccer/football field at

McGill University to watch the Rugby games taking place.

If she could make it until October 28 without having any seizures or major issues, the institute would release her to go home. As the days went on, she got better and stronger. Maria already had visions and plans for even the simplest of pleasure for when she returned home. ***"People were asking me constantly as to what I would do upon returning home. Besides kissing and hugging all of my loved ones, I actually looked forward to taking a shower alone, with no one having to watch over me and make sure I didn't collapse with a seizure. I also looked forward to taking my boys on a walk alone outside. Things people took for granted, I looked forward to doing for the first time seizure-free. I had been gone for six weeks already and ready to come home.***

A plane ride home might be scary, but after fighting to be a normal wife, mother and every day normal human being like the millions around me, a plane ride was the least of my concerns or worries. I looked forward to holding Vince, he was 19 months old and I had never held him by myself. My sweet Donald had already gone through so much at the age of five, I wanted to show him it was all going to be okay. That plane could not land fast enough. I wanted Donald to see that through belief in God, anything was possible.

As the plane landed in Cleveland, the staff was aware of my prior issues and insisted that I get in a wheelchair. I begged them to let me walk off the plane and not be wheeled out because I wanted my family to see me on my feet and okay. As I walked through the tunnel off the plane, I saw my entire family standing there. My son Donald ran to me with tears in his eyes and told me he loved me, and asked me never to leave him again. Vince just looked at me with a puzzled look; he still didn't realize who I was, and instead just went right back into his Grandmother's arms. We celebrated back at my parent's house with good food, God and family."

Maria's family sat around her and peppered her with questions about her experience in Canada and how life was seizure-free. Baby Vince stayed his distance, not sure what to think of the bald women in front of him he had barely seen in his very young life. Once Maria finally convinced her son to come to her, he would need constant reassurance that everything was okay. He insisted on touching her face on the right side because it sagged, and would continue to sag until all the muscles in her head grew stronger. Vince looked up at his mom with a quizzical look, his blonde hair slicked back and his big brown eyes open wide; he simply didn't know what to make of it. It didn't take long for Vince to climb down and run back to one of his aunts. The first two years are crucial for mother-child bonding, and Maria and Vince would have a lot of catching up to do.

Maria reflects back on the first meal back home with her whole family surrounding her: ***"My mom made spaghetti and meatballs with homemade bread. I hadn't had a meal that good since I left two months earlier. I ate until I couldn't move. My mom made the best sauce in the world. She taught all of us sisters how to make it.***

I had missed so much while I was gone: my brother James got engaged to his girlfriend, Elsa. It was exciting because the family was continuing to grow. My other brother Joey had gotten married a few months before I left for Canada, and he had just found out him and his wife Karen were expecting a baby. It was exciting because our family was going to have two new additions. I was finally going to be able to enjoy life and watch my boys grow and my family at peace. Knowing that I was going to be alive and normal was the most awesome feeling imaginable.

We left my parents house and drove home. It only took three minutes because it was just two blocks away. When we pulled in the driveway, I looked at my little house and began to cry. I never thought I'd see it again. My neighbors Tom and Jimmy Lou were there waiting

to greet me and celebrate. They gave me a giant hug and kiss, and it was so nice to be home and be around those who had done so much for me. I had gone 52 days without a seizure, and I was thankful to God for my new lease on life and the miracle given to me."

When Maria walked in her house, she saw a giant stack of get well cards on the table. The freezer and fridge were filled with food from friends, family and neighbors. As she soaked in the comfort of being home and healthy for the first time in her life, the phone rang. Snapping her out of her euphoria was Don jumping to answer the phone before Maria could lapse into a seizure. Something was different this time, however: Maria was completely fine. Her body wasn't jerking, her eyes weren't twitching and she didn't have anything close to a seizure. The miracle that Dr. Feindel performed was shining through loud and clear. This point was even clearer when moments later Maria went to the bathroom by herself with no assistance and no one waiting by the door, waiting to help at a second's notice.

Everyone began to adjust to her new lifestyle, one without constant fear and pain affecting her every mood. Maria was able to convince her mother that she didn't need to bring her over her house everyday and watch her, but allowed her to be alone with Vince and be a mommy for him while Donald was at school. Maria enjoyed every second of it, as she was able to get Donald ready for school in the morning for the first time all by herself.

Vince was still struggling with the concept of having a mother. He called Maria mommy only seldom, and with hesitation when he did. Most times when he needed something he would call out for his grandma or one of his aunts, even when they weren't there. One day after Donald went to school and Maria was left alone with Vince, tragedy almost struck. Maria laid him down in his crib for a nap and believed he had fallen fast asleep. Maria loaded the dishwasher in the kitchen and then went and sat on the couch when she heard the water in the bathroom running.

The house was small enough for Maria to get into the bathroom in only mere seconds, but it was too late. Vince was naked and sitting in the bath tub with the scalding hot water filling it up. He looked up at his mother and said, ***"Hey lady, I'm taking a bath!"*** He was only 22 months old but quick and strong, and was easily able to climb out of his crib and into the bathroom. Maria looks back at that scary ordeal: ***"I knew God was with me as I pulled him from the tub. He didn't start screaming until his body hit the cold air and began to scab. I ran him over to my neighbors' house where I knew they always kept a freezer of ice. I kicked it open and sat Vince in it so the ice would cool down his butt and back that were burning up. I quickly told Jimmy Lou to call 911 and she did. It was November 3rd, and I was freezing, I had no shoes on and was standing in the snow waiting for the ambulance to arrive."***

When the ambulance arrived, the paramedics saw Maria first, shaved head, contorted face and though it was her that needed the help. Maria quickly explained it was her son that needed the ambulance and not her. The paramedics wrapped Vince up in bubble wrap and placed him in the back of the ambulance. They first took Vince to Fairview hospital but realized by the time they arrived to keep him in the ambulance and transport him to the Metro Hospital Burn unit instead.

Maria was just starting to know her baby. Her oldest son Donald didn't even start walking until he was 14 months, and never caused any trouble or got into anything, as a toddler Donald was always at his mother's side. Vince, on the other hand, was completely different, as he started walking at 8 months and getting into everything. At 22 months old, Vince was lightning fast and smart, and could do pretty much anything; Maria was unaware and didn't realize the giant challenge she was undertaking.

When the ambulance carrying Vince arrived at Metro, Don and the DeLuca family were there waiting for Vince and Maria. Jimmy Lou had phoned them and they rushed there. Don was able to register the information needed at the front desk in regards to medical history; Maria, however, was taken away by social workers to question her as to what exactly happened. They bombarded Maria with questions, and didn't believe her look and demeanor was from brain surgery. Those types of surgeries weren't performed yet in America and the social workers did not believe anything Maria was trying to tell them. Sadly, this was an age in time were drug addicts were hurting their children on purpose, and Maria looked like something between an addict and a mental patient because of the shaved head and contorted face.

Maria reflects back: ***"So many people hurt their children. I never would because I loved Vince. I kept telling them that and asking for them to bring in my husband and parents, saying they could answer the questions I couldn't. I was just getting to know Vince, but they said they wanted to know what I knew and how this could happen. I just wanted to see if he was okay, and I wanted my husband and parents with me. I was so scared and they were trying to make me say I placed him in the hot water on purpose. It took three hours of convincing them that I didn't do it on purpose until they let me go to be with my son and family. I felt so bad because in the 7 years of my marriage with Don, I spent more time in a hospital bed then I did in bed with him."***

When they finally let Maria see Vince, he was behind glass and she had to look at him through a window. Vince had suffered from 3rd degree burns on his feet and the bottom of his butt. By placing him in the ice, Maria helped prevent him from having to have skin craft surgery. The first week he was in recovery at the hospital they would not let Maria touch him. She could only see him through a window. She had already been through so much and just wanted to be a mother to Vince. She wanted what most women are able to take for granted.

This was hard on Donald, as well. At six years old, his eyes continued to see the horror that most people who live to be 80 years old do not even see. He was allowed to visit his brother after the first week, but it wasn't the same as having Vince home with him. It wasn't until December 17, 1983 - almost 6 weeks later - that Vince was allowed to come home from the burn unit and join his family. The doctors and nurses had to train Don and Maria how to change his special bandages without making the damage worse. It was 8 days before Christmas, and the McKees were finally whole again.

Don and Maria took Vince and Donald to see Santa at the mall. Christmas was now less than a week away, but they knew it was important and worth dealing with the last second crowd. When Santa Claus asked Donald what he wanted for Christmas, he told Santa, ***"I have my mommy and my brother home and that is all I wanted."*** Donald said all of this with tears in his eyes. Santa looked over at Maria and could tell something was wrong; she had a large scar across a bald head with maybe an inch of hair on her head. Her face was still sagging, as well. That's when Don and Maria interjected and told Santa that he should bring Donald a Dukes of Hazzard Big Wheel because he was such a good little boy and big brother.

That Christmas Eve was extra special, as Maria was home and healthy, and it was her first as a healthy mother. Vince was starting to get to be old enough to realize what was going on, and it was very special for the McKee family. Everyone was at the DeLuca house, as tradition always had it. The night would always begin with Mass at St. Patrick's and then dinner at the DeLucas. Maria looks back on that peaceful and joyous night: ***"It was the first Christmas I had without seizures. When a bell or buzzer from a toy would go off, right away everyone would look at me and get ready to help, but this year they didn't need too, I was fine. My entire family was smiling ear to ear as everyone was starting to realize for the first time in my life, I was fine."***

Another small miracle happened the next morning on Christmas day:

"When I opened the door Christmas morning to grab the newspaper I quickly noticed my front porch was loaded with presents and a basket of food. I woke Don and we wondered where it all came from. The note on the package read, 'A gift from Jesus.' There was a gift for each one of us and a couple of outfits for both Donald and Vince. We only had enough money to buy them each a few gifts because of all the money we had to put out that year on traveling to Canada and the never ending hospital bills, so these added gifts from whoever the kind stranger was, really helped fill underneath the tree."

Life was slowly starting to come together once and for all for Maria and the next several years were proof that if you have faith, work hard and never stop believing, miracles can happen. By the fall of 1987, Donald was in the second grade and Vince was getting ready to start kindergarten at St. Patrick's. At this time, they only sent kids to kindergarten for half of a day; Vince was scheduled to be in the morning class. Each day would start off with mass in the morning, then dropping both boys of at school. With Maria not able to drive (yet), Rosemarie would come buy and pick them all up so the boys would have a ride and not have to walk.

A few months into the school year, the children and teachers noticed that Maria had a gift and was genuinely happy to be around children and help whenever she could. A few of the teachers asked Maria to stay at the school after she dropped Vince off and help grade papers and just be a part of things. Mrs. Geromes, the kindergarten teacher, asked Maria to stay on as a full time aide with her classes. Maria was doing everything from grading papers to teaching children how to count and tie their shoes.

This was also the first time in her life she had the chance to show off her artwork and drawing ability. There was a popular show the school children loved called the "Letter People". The show was packed with 26 colorful characters representing each letter of the alphabet. Maria was asked to draw each character on large pieces of poster board for the Kindergarten class to have. Years after she begged to take art classes and was told no, her artistic ability was finally allowed to break through. Maria just wasn't living life, she was living to inspire! Every step she took was progress; every day without a seizure was a miracle!

Maria was breaking down walls that she had faced her entire life, climbing the mountains of life and defeating challenges every day. She still had a few goals in mind to achieve, things that numerous people - including logic - told her she would never accomplish, one of which was driving a car.

The date was set for January 27, 1988, a routine Wednesday for most Americans, but for Maria, a day set to further define her destiny. Maria started the day in Vince's kindergarten class with Mrs. Geromes and all the children. Her long awaited test wasn't until 9:30 am, at a location five minutes from the school. The class was excited for Maria and drew her pictures of her driving a car. It was a sweet gesture and also helped calm her nerves. Other teachers made a point of stopping by the class to wish Maria luck, as well. Her legacy was growing, and those who knew of it were completely behind her.

It wasn't long before the school nurse, Mrs. Welsh, came to the room to let Maria know it was time to go. Rosemarie was there to pick up her daughter and bring her to her date with destiny at Puritas DMV. Rosemarie had been saying several rosaries all morning in preparation for Maria's big test. Maria told the children that if she passed, she would come back and see them all to celebrate.

Maria and Rosemarie were only at the Puritas DMV for about 10 minutes before she was called back for her test with the instructor. The test was quick, partial road, partial parking; she passed both with flying colors and another part of the dream was complete. Maria explains here her emotions at the time as this next milestone was achieved: ***"I was 32 years old and I felt like I was 16. My mother knew I passed the test just by looking at the smile on my face as I walked out of the building.***

That first doctor I had who always told me I would never be able to drive, or do so many others things - I just proved him wrong again! I got stronger and more confident that I could do anything I set my mind to do. Between driving, being a mommy and a wife, combined with all the hours I got to volunteer at the school, I was getting to do all the things I had dreamt about my entire life "

Rosemarie DeLuca drove her daughter back to St. Patrick's so Maria could share the good news with both of her sons. As Maria arrived in the parking lot, she noticed Vince's entire class standing outside with a big sign that said, "Congratulations Mrs. McKee". The class also had flowers to give to her and a small St. Christopher metal.

Four days after getting her driver's license, Maria was still buzzing with excitement, but sports fans everywhere were buzzing with excitement that day for a different reason: it was Super Bowl XXII between the Washington Redskins and Denver Broncos. The game was very memorable because after trailing 10–0 at the end of the first quarter of Super Bowl XXII, the Redskins scored 42 unanswered points, including a record-breaking 35 points in the second quarter, and setting several other Super Bowl records. Williams, who was named the Super Bowl MVP, completed 18 of 29 passes for a Super Bowl record 340 yards and four touchdowns, with one interception. He also became the first player in Super Bowl history to pass for four touchdowns in a single quarter, and four in a half. Williams was the first African American starting quarterback to win a Super Bowl. The 10-point deficit remains the largest deficit overcome by a Super Bowl winning team.

While the night will be remembered by many as a classic Super Bowl performance by Williams and the Redskins, the night will be remembered by Maria McKee and family for a completely different reason. Lisa Cartelone of Channel 8 news in Cleveland heard of Maria's incredible story and knew that it would make the perfect news piece. So, the day of the Super Bowl, the channel 8 news cast team came to the home of Maria

McKee and family, and told her story for all to see in Northeast Ohio. Those who stayed up after the Super Bowl to watch the news got to see and hear about Maria's epic tale. It was further proof of how incredible her story was that it could lead off the newscast over the Super Bowl.

The next two plus years went great for Maria and the McKee family. The seizures never returned, and she got to be an active part of her family's lives. She continued to help out at St. Patrick's, and also got to attend all of her sons' little league baseball games and other special occasions. Because of the upturn in her health, she was even able to throw birthday parties for her children. This may seem like everyday stuff for most mothers, but for Maria it was a joy she never thought she could have. So many things that were taken for granted by many were celebrations of life for Maria. It was a wonderful two plus years filled with happy memories.

In the spring of 1990, the McKee's put their house up for sale in West Park. The boys were getting older and the neighborhood was starting to decline. They also knew that it wouldn't be too many more years before the City of Cleveland bought out their house and the others around it to start getting ready to expand the land by Cleveland Hopkins Airport, a location just three streets over from Midvale, from which they lived.

The house sold in a fair amount of time, and it allowed them to purchase a home in North Olmsted, Ohio; a location only 8 minutes away from their current residence, but in many ways a city that almost seemed worlds apart from what they were used to.

As the boys adjusted to their new schools Maple Elementary and North Olmsted Middle School, Maria looked to help out with the PTA and with other such functions, as she did at St. Patrick's. Maria would quickly learn that the culture of attitude in North Olmsted was drastically different than those which she encountered in Cleveland. At her very first PTA meeting, a simple hello was not given to her from any of the other mothers who had been attending North Olmsted PTA for years. Instead, Maria was mocked from being from Cleveland, and many of the other mothers thought it was a joke. They told her not worry about being in the PTA, but rather to focus on the janitorial department. It was mockery by those who lived their life based on money and not God.

Like so many times prior in her life, Maria took this minus and made it a plus, as she used the time she would have spent on the PTA and instead went to beauty school. One of her dreams was to be a beautician; however, because of the epilepsy, she was never able to pursue it in any way. Times were different now, the seizures were gone, both boys were in school full time and the window of opportunity was wide open.

A few weeks after the debacle at the North Olmsted PTA meeting, with some of the mothers from little league eating wine and fancy cheese instead of peanuts and soda pop, Maria turned to her local phone book and found McLords Beauty Academy. Moments later, Maria was on the phone signing up. Classes were to start January 7, 1991, and this gave Maria enough time to raise the money needed to attend the school, which cost a healthy $7,500 fee.

The fee was well worth it, as Maria loved the school and made the most of her opportunity at achieving another dream. She was the oldest of the 12 students in her class, and the others kindly referred to her as "mom". The nickname came in handy when people in class where trying to get a hold of her in the room, because there was actually several other Marias in the class.

The course was intense and took 1800 hours to complete, roughly 18 - 24 months. Maria took classes seven and half hours a day, for five days a week, and also spent several ten hour Saturdays at the school to earn her degree. She was determined, and as she learned more and grew more comfortable she increased the time she was at the school, increasing weekdays to ten hours a day and even some eighteen-hour Saturdays. The time flew by and it was December 18, 1991 when she completed the course and began studying to pass her state boards.

The state board test was January 7, 1992, about three weeks away. Maria used the time over the holidays to study hard and work on her craft. The day of the test she took her niece, Frances, and Don with her down to Columbus for the exam. Columbus is two hours south of North Olmsted, so they traveled down the night before and stayed at a local motel for the night. Frances was there because Maria would need a hair model to work on. She stayed up all night the evening before the test practicing on Frances, while Don quizzed her with questions for the written part of the test. The following day, the entire day of testing took ten hours and it was dark outside by the time it wrapped up for the day.

The boys were off of school for another week following her test because of Christmas break wrapping up and, because of that, Don took the week off, as well. Maria enjoyed the quality time with her family but also kept a close eye on the mailbox for those test results to show up. No time table was given on when they would arrive, but Maria was well equipped at the crucial virtue of patience.

As the days passed the tension grew, and Maria wondered what the mailman would bring and when he would bring it. It was the Saturday following the test, and Don got up very early and went to the post office. He couldn't wait any longer, and he convinced the post office to let him have the piece of mail for his wife. Luckily it happened to be there, and Don was able to secure it.

Maria knew what Don was doing, and waited idly for him to return home. The rumor was that if the results showed up in an envelope with a window, you failed and would have to retake the test. If it was a solid envelope, then you passed. Maria explains how this myth ended up being debunked, and the emotion of finding out the actual test results: ***"Don got up early and went to the post office when they opened in the morning. He didn't return for two plus hours, and it had me nervous because I feared he didn't want to return home with bad news. I just stayed calm and sat on the couch praying the rosary. When***

Don returned, he had a bouquet of roses with him; he also had an envelope with a window in it. I started to cry."

Despite the rumor of the dreaded window envelope meaning failure, the myth was proven false, as Maria actually did pass! She received a 78% on the hair cut portion, a 95% on the hands-on portion and a 100% on the written test. She even took the test that would allow her to manage a beauty shop, and received a 92% on that, as well. She passed everything and received both her beautician's license and her manager's license.

At 37 years old, Maria was continuing to break down barriers and realize dreams. If it wasn't for the miracle in Montreal and the constant belief in herself and her lord and savior, Maria would have never been able to reach the goals that most thought were impossible. She was married in 1976, became a mother in 1978, a mother again in 1982, beat epilepsy by surviving a miracle brain surgery in 1983, became a licensed motorist in 1988, and a licensed beautician in 1992 - a sixteen-year stretch that most people wouldn't be able to achieve in sixty years, let alone someone who was forced to live with a disability her whole life until the surgery.

The next years of her life were also incredible. She got to live the dream being a beautician, and her excellent work ethic combined with enthusiasm for her job allowed her to rise through the ranks and mange her own shop. The McKees were still not rich with money, as the medical bills would last a lifetime, but the riches they had in love were immeasurable by any dollar amount.

Vince started high school in the fall of 1996 while Don graduated high school in the spring of 1997. Maria also continued to give back to the community and church and became an active member in the St. Brendan's Youth Group. She also became a Eucharistic minister at the church, sat on the parish council and even taught PSR classes. She organized the altar rosary group at the church, as well as helped out with Bingo kitchen. Shortly after that she began cooking for the priests at her church as well, one of her many talents. Just like years prior at St. Patrick's, she was once again a major part of a church, and she loved it.

It was also during this time of Donald's graduation year that Maria once again received the chance at redemption. It had been seven years since the McKee family moved from Cleveland to North Olmsted, and seven years since the snooty women of the North Olmsted self-appointed upper echelon mocked Maria for her origins. Times had changed mightily, as the theme of the 1997 North Olmsted After Prom was Tropical Casino night, and there was only one women qualified to draw the giant playing cards being used for decorations.

Maria reflects back on Donald's after prom and also her chance to show those same women what she was made of: ***"Coming off of my surgery and everything else going on with my body, I very easily could have just rested, but I knew this was important and I had a passion for it. I was excited to come home from the initial after prom planning meeting and tell Don all about it. I had been voted co-Chair of the decorating committee that night, as well. Don was smart enough to realize what this meant and, sure enough, over the next six months our basement and garage was filled with homemade palm trees and giant playing cards. It was quite the scene, as I also had been doing hair out of my basement, so it was like having a mixture of beauty shop in a fake tropical paradise. It was a fun time for sure."***

The decorations turned out great and it truly was sweet redemption for Maria. The students at the after prom loved the scenery, and Maria was very proud of her work. She saw many of the same young women that evening at After Prom who had been coming over to the house to get their hair done earlier in the week and pretty much all school year. Maria almost never charged the young girls to do their hair, but rather did it as a goodwill gesture. She never had any daughters, so she relished the chance to do makeup and hair for the teenage girls. Donald and Vince didn't mind the girls coming over the house, either.

A couple of years later, with Vince a junior in high school and an active member in the North Olmsted Acapella show choir, Maria once again had her chance to show off her artistic ability. As part of a fundraiser to raise money for a trip the choir was taking to Disney to perform at Epcot Center, the group needed to put on a Christmas musical complete with colorful outfits and Christmas decorations. Maria and Don were both a natural fit to help, and enjoyed doing so. Maria would often look back during these times and once again thank God for the chance not only to see her son perform in musicals, but also be healthy enough to help. Once again, it was her artwork that she got to show off, a talent that had been stifled for so many years. Things for Maria would continue to get better as the years went on.

It was June 22, 2002, and Maria had endured so much to make it to that day. She explains just how incredible it felt to reach that point in her life: ***"The day Donald got married was one of the happiest of my life. He started off in this world struggling to live, and with prayers and God he made it through. Seeing him mature and become the strong God loving man he is was such a blessing. I loved his new wife Abbie, she was perfect for Donald.***

As I watched Donald wait for his beautiful bride to come down the aisle, I thanked God for getting me to this day. If I listened to the doctors, then Donald would have never been born. I may have died, but it was worth it to give birth to him. I cried so many tears of joy that day as Fr. Steve Moran and Fr. Murray performed the mass."

Several years later, Don and Abbie would help Maria realize another dream when they delivered to her her first grandchild, a beautiful baby boy named Matthew who brought incredible joy to the entire McKee family.

Full of life and energy and with an attitude of anything being possible, Maria continued to tackle goals and challenges she had dreamt about her entire life. Her next feat was to start her own catering company. She placed the hair cutting gig on hold and put her full focus on cooking. Maria discusses how this unique transition began: ***"I found myself settling down in my older age, but wanted to continue doing things I loved. I found myself cooking a lot for people's parties. Each time, the events got bigger and better. I eventually started cooking my own created dishes for retirement parties, office parties and even weddings. I started cooking for several church functions, as well. Every time I turned around I found myself cooking more and more.***

After months passed with me cooking for everyone and everything, I decided to open up my own catering company called Maria's Catering. It was so much fun, as my nephew Tony Warmuth helped me put together menus and advertisements. "

It was the catering that led Maria to discover one of the greatest joys her life would ever have. That joy was the "Homeless Stand Down". The Homeless Stand Down (HSD) is a two-day event for individuals and families facing poverty and homelessness. On day one, guests enjoy access to social service providers, haircuts, medical screenings, live entertainment, professional portraits, breakfast and lunch, free winter clothing, personal care kits, bus passes and much more. During day two of the event, the homeless in attendance experience many of the same services, the difference being that after the event the bagged lunches, winter clothing, etc. are packaged into a CareVan and driven to guest's permanent supportive housing sites around Greater Cleveland. She saw a sign at St. Brendan's notifying people their need for volunteers to cook turkeys for the event. She didn't hesitate to help cook all 20 turkeys and deliver them to the site along with fresh fruit and cookies. As she arrived at the site, a group of homeless men came straight to her, asking for the food. As she looked around, she saw hundreds of homeless standing around and knew that she needed to do something. She knew she couldn't just leave without helping in some way.

Maria explains how she was overcome by the moment: ***"I asked one***

of the workers how I could help, and he had me come into Public Hall. I saw all the doctors, social workers and so many other professionals there to help the homeless. They had someone there for every service possible, with the exception of haircuts. I knew that it was God calling me to be there and lend my help. Within an hour, I returned with all my hair cutting supplies - including ones I had stopped off and bought on the way home - and was ready to do my part in helping these souls in need. As Jesus said, as you do on to the least of your brothers, you do to me."

Upon her return to Public Hall, there was over 50 men in line already waiting on her for a haircut. Over the next 7 hours, Maria would cut over 70 heads of hair, but there was still a large group of people waiting. The event was about to end for the day, but Maria wasted no time in assuring Tony Veto, the main organizer of the event, that she would return the next day as well to finish cutting for everyone. Not only did Maria volunteer for day two, but also gave her time the next four weekends, as well. By the time the fourth weekend was complete, Maria had given out a total of 627 haircuts.

Over the next decade, Maria would be a strong presence at the Stand Down. In October of 2009, she was awarded the Humanitarian of the Year Award, as well as the Special Volunteer of the Year Award by the committee in charge of the Stand Down. Later that year, the Holy Name Society honored her with the Holy Spirit Award. She was also honored as the Person of the Week by the Suns News Herald. Her outstanding efforts in the field of philanthropy were being recognized.

With everything going well for Maria in her work with the homeless, the lord blessed her again with another daughter-in-law. This time it was her youngest son Vince getting married to his long-time girlfriend, Emily. Two years into their marriage, they brought more joy into the heart of Maria, as they made her a grandmother again with the addition of their newborn daughter, Maggie. Maria talks about the joy of being a grandmother and, coincidentally enough, that her son Vince and daughter in law Emily live only seven houses down, so she gets to see plenty of her granddaughter, Maggie: ***"My legs melt when I hold her, she is so beautiful and smart. Don and I are so blessed to live so close to her. I get to watch her several times a week while they are at work and it is great. It is tough with Matthew, my grandson, because they (Donald and Abbie) live so far away in North Carolina that I don't get to see him very often.***

It is incredible with Maggie because I get to watch her grow right in front of my eyes. She calls me 'Maga' and I love it. God has blessed me with so many wonderful people in my life and I'm very grateful. All I ever wanted to do was have a normal life, and because I never gave up I got to accomplish all of my dreams, including being a mommy and now a grandmother."

As for Dr. Stone, the man who claimed Maria would never have a life or find happiness, she has a message for him: ***" I would like to take that man a picture of my children, husband and now grandchildren, along with my high school diploma, driver's license, beautician's license, volunteer awards, and lay it all on his desk for him to look at. I did it, I proved him wrong"***

Maria insists that, ***"When you have faith in God, anything and everything is possible. When you're willing to carry some of the crosses he gives you, look at the blessing he gives you in return.***

The advice I would give others that suffer from epilepsy would be to never give up. There is hope out there. Never let a doctor tell you that you can't believe in yourself and in God. If you want it bad enough, it can happen. The seizures can stop. Don't let a seizure stop you from believing you can do anything.

Patients suffering from epilepsy need to ask their doctors about McGill University and this wonderful hospital that saved my life. Every neurology doctor knows about this school and hospital. They

study the brain and know more about it than anyone else in the world. Search for real answers and don't just let them dope you up with medicine. I realize we all live in fear every day of the next big seizure, but it is not worth being doped up every day. Instead, find an answer. It wasn't too long ago I was waking up from seizures, looking at people laughing at me and wondering where the hell I was at. Don't take no for an answer; you can and will find help."

What would Maria say to the people of McGill University who saved her life? She tells all of us here: ***"I would love to one day be able to go up there and thank everyone of the doctors, nurses and fellow patients. I want to thank everyone associated with the hospital. God bless those people for giving me a new life, because they cared and were working for a cure, not working for money. Those people took care of everyone in a genuine way and took on a lot of responsibility doing it. "***

The journey of Maria McKee was so incredibly unique and filled with challenges that no one would have blamed her for giving up numerous times throughout the life of ordeals that came her way. Not only didn't she give up, but once the surgery was complete in Montreal, she didn't rest on her laurels; instead she went after lifelong goals that were once seen as impossible.

What makes things even more impressive in my book - and this is my book - is the fact that not only did she live a normal life, but she made time to help others who were struggling, as well. In the day and age we live, where so many people are obsessed with taking selfies and checking their Facebook posts, it is refreshing to see a person not obsessed with self-image and glorification, but rather a person who wants to give back to Christ in the same way a new life was given to her.

Chapter Seven

WHEN DESTINY CHANGES COURSE

> *"You can't control the cards you're dealt but you can control your attitude and your resiliency to bounce back. That is how winners are made."*
>
> ***Lana***

Vonda Ward is best known for being an athlete, and this book was intended to honor those outside of the sports world. However, when I had the chance to meet Vonda Ward the person, I quickly realized that as great as her in ring career was, she is an even better person outside of the ring. Her story is one of courage, hope and the ability to adapt when life throws you a curveball. Thus, I felt it would be a perfect fit for this book.

I first met Vonda back in 2004 at a body building show. She stopped what she was doing and took a picture with me. At the time, I was nothing more than a 22-year-old kid wanting to meet a celebrity. 11 years later, I had the privilege to meet her again, as she sat with me at a book signing for my book featuring her entitled Ohio Warriors and helped raise a ton of money for charity that evening. She is an incredible human being, and I truly feel that when people read this chapter they will realize exactly why I included it. She truly is a woman who lives every day of her life to inspire and help others! This is the story of Vonda Ward the person, not just the athlete.

When sports fans think of two-sport athletes, they commonly think of Deon Sanders or Bo Jackson, both of who played in the NFL and MLB in the 1990's to great success. Seldom do we think of women as two-sport athletes. It is a narrow thought by many that a woman can't be as good at sports as a man; it's a thought that is naive and wrong. Long before the world of MMA and Boxing had Ronda Rousey to hang its hat on as the world's toughest woman, it had Vonda Ward, a true two-sport superstar who has never taken a single day of her life for granted.

She was destined for basketball greatness when a life event she couldn't avoid changed everything in her path. She didn't cry, she didn't blame anyone, she simply went with the left turn destiny gave her and proved why she is one of the greatest athletes in modern day sports. Vonda Ward is a hero, a warrior and a woman who proved she could do anything a man could do, if not better and with more heart.

Born on March 16, 1973, Ward grew up in Macedonia, Ohio. She was surrounded by sports at a young age, as her dad, Larry Ward, was a famous harness racer at Northfield Park. She didn't get to become too attached with her father, however, because of his busy work schedule at Northfield Racetrack. Her parents divorced at the age of 10 and he moved away to Washington DC. It wasn't until her mid-thirties that Vonda was able to fully re-unite with her father. It happened in enough time for her to say goodbye, as her father died soon after from lung cancer.

Because of this, she became very close with her mom, Roseann, who was working three jobs to raise her. Roseann worked very hard to keep a roof over her daughter's head and food on the table. It was a strong bond between mother and daughter that would last a life time and mold

Vonda's life in many ways. Vonda was always involved in sports and, even juggling three jobs, Roseann made every attempt to be at every single game and practice to support her daughter.

Even on the days when Roseann was exhausted after work, she would still make time to spend with her daughter in the backyard working on her basketball game. They would play soccer, as well. Because of Vonda's height, she was typically the goalie, so Roseann would fire shots at her to help improve. She was a mom, a mentor and a best friend for Vonda. It didn't matter if Roseann was running on four hours of sleep, she was there to help and support her daughter.

When the Ward women weren't working on jump shots and saves, they were out in nature, as they both loved to be in the great outdoors. They enjoyed hiking, biking and being outside as much as they possibly could be. It was the hard work ethic instilled in Vonda from her mother at a young age that helped her grow up to become the woman she did. With a father who left at ten years old and a mother who worked three jobs, Vonda could have complained and wasted away her life feeling sorry for herself. Instead, she busted her tail and became a star athlete.

Vonda talks a little bit about growing up and who inspired her along the way: ***"I had a true love and passion for any sport growing up. I was a natural born athlete. The people who helped along the way are the numerous coaches I've had in sports since age five. The most important people who helped me along the way were my mom and both grandmas, who supported me. My grandmas would always be out practicing with me when I was little and my mom has always been an inspiration in my life. She showed me how hard work and perseverance leads to success in life. Since there were not many women's professional sports when I was growing up, I really didn't have any particular athletes that I looked up to except for Michael Jordan. "***

Despite being as good as she was at multiple sports growing up, she never took it for granted that she would be a pro athlete one day. ***"When I was growing up, there really wasn't many pro sports women could play. It really wasn't something I thought about being a sure thing or something that would happen. I knew I could always to play in college, but it wasn't until I got out of college that I realized I could take it to the professional level. People always respected me for my abilities, and I think that is because they saw how hard I worked. If you work hard, your actions will say it all. I showed respect to everyone around me, and if you give it, you should get it."***

It was no secret that Roseann was her daughter's hero, but it was also Roseann's mother - Vonda's grandmother - that would provide incredible inspiration throughout Vonda's life. Her grandmother was only 34 when she got jaw cancer, with very little to no treatment known in those days to fix it. Instead of chemo and radiation that were still light years away at the time, doctors chose to remove her jaw as part of 15 different surgeries, and she was told she only had a year to live when she was still in her thirties. She defied the odds and lived into her 90's, dying when she was 92. Even before Vonda dribbled a single basketball or threw a jab, her grandmother was blazing a trail of living a legacy to inspire.

Before she ever stepped into a boxing ring, Vonda Ward's first love was basketball. She played at Trinity High School in Garfield Heights, and was twice named Ohio's "Ms. Basketball." She was voted onto the Parade All American teams twice in her high school career, as well. Despite being the number-one ranked player and recruit in the nation, her mother always kept her grounded and humble. Roseann was a great role model for Vonda and never allowed her to develop an ego or get a big head. She always kept things in perspective for Vonda.

So impressive was Ward in high school on the court that she was recruited by Division I universities all across the United States. Despite the large amount of options, the choice was easy for Ward, as she accepted a scholarship to play with the most prestigious program in women's college basketball, the University of Tennessee. She wanted to play for Hall of Fame women's coach Pat Summitt. Ward goes on to talk more about the decision to attend Tennessee: ***"I decided to go to Tennessee to challenge myself and to play for one of the greatest coaches in college basketball, and also to be part of a winning tradition."***

It was also during this time that her popularity on a national level grew. She was very respected and loved. Unlike some sports stars who seem to forget the fans at the first sniff of success, Ward never forgot where she came from and continued to live by the golden rule of treating people with respect. She explains why the fans and the respect she had for them was so important: ***"I always think whatever sport or whatever you do, if you excel at it, you have to act like you're the best. But once you step out of that environment, you must act like everyone else and show respect. You have to stay humble and treat others well. I always took time for fans because where would I be without them? If there are no fans, then you're going to be playing and fighting in empty arenas. It is important to be gracious to everyone."***

The choice was a wise one as, during her college career at Tennessee, she got the coveted chance to play for a National Championship in 1995. The outcome was not what she had hoped for, as they lost to fellow dominant basketball college, the University of Connecticut.

While at college, her love of competition and desire to win only began to grow, as she competed with USA Basketball as a member of the 1993 Jones Cup Team that won the Bronze in Taipei. It was her first taste of national exposure, and she loved it! Because of her love for international competition, after her college career ended in 1995, Ward played for a professional basketball club in Germany. She eventually returned back to the United States, where she played for the American Basketball League's Colorado Xplosion.

Ward talked a little bit about having to go overseas after college to play professional basketball, as well as how it felt to eventually return to the United States and get to play professionally in her home country, as well: ***"When I first came out of college, we had no professional women's basketball in the United States. It was a dream come true to play pro basketball in the USA and to be a member of the first league that provided the opportunity for women to be able to continue their professional basketball career here in the USA."***

Despite her basketball career ending prematurely when the league folded, the desire to win and compete burned strong inside of her. She decided to take up boxing because of her gigantic size and her love to compete. Ward stood at 6 foot 6 inches, and would hold a serious reach advantage against almost any opponent. She met her trainer Lorenzo Scott, and things took off from there.

A lot of people would have been bitter or looked for someone to blame for their career ending shortly, but Vonda wasn't that way. She grew up knowing that with hard work and respect that anything was possible. She was also a women of faith, and knew that her life in sports was destined to continue, just this time in a ring and not on a court.

Ward explains the decision to turn to boxing, and also the process of transition that comes with it: ***"When I was a young girl, I was interested in boxing; I even had a punching bag hanging in my room growing up. It was something I was always interested in. Basketball was still my first true love, of course, playing it from the time I was five years old to the time I was 23 or 24; then I got hurt. I just started using boxing as a way to stay in shape, and we took things from there.***

When I met Lorenzo Scott, I believe it was meant to be and a blessing. He's one of the best trainers in the area, so when he told me he saw potential, I trusted him and soon my boxing career began."

Famed trainer Ed King - also owner of King's Gym - will be the first to tell you that women's boxing can be more exciting then men's at times, as he explains here: ***"I think the main difference between male***

boxing and female boxing is that women tend to try harder. When I go to a fight card as a judge or referee, I know that the female boxing matches tend to be more exciting because they just seem to put more effort into it, and it is usually non-stop action. I believe the reason they try harder is that they feel they have something to prove and that they need to prove they deserve to be on the card. That held true for Vonda in her career as well, because no matter where she was on the card, her fights were always the most exciting. "

Vonda was no stranger to hard work and a big challenge. She would have one on her hands when it came to stepping in the ring. Her typical days of training consisted of waking up before the sun rise and going on a five mile run before returning to gym to train some of her personal training clients. After training other clients, she would do her own training with weights and strength and conditioning exercises and routines. Her afternoons were spent traveling to Akron for more training, this time in the ring, perfecting her craft.

The long days of training were one thing, but, like with any great athlete, no amount of success comes without sacrifice. Ward was no exception, as she sacrificed a lot to get her career off the ground. She talks about some of the sacrifices and challenges she faced to get her boxing career underway and stay successful: ***"There is a lot of sacrifice that comes with being a professional athlete. It is all worth it if you are doing something you love and you have the ability to excel at it and set your mind and heart to it. You always need people around you who are going to support you. I have been blessed with a great set of friends and family to support me, and you need that more than anything."***

Her boxing career began on January 15, 2000, when she knocked out Faye Steffen in round one at LaPorte, Indiana. It was a dominant victory that saw Ward win in only 24 seconds. This brutal victory also sent Steffen into permanent retirement from the ring. Ward explains the thrill of securing her first win, let alone so quickly: ***"When I won my first fight by knockout in 24 seconds, I was hooked on the sport, and it gave me confidence to continue."***

This was the first of four straight first round knockouts to start her career. The second knockout victory came against Mattie Brumley at one minute and twenty seconds into the first round. It was part of a card at the Indiana State Fairgrounds in Indianapolis on February 29, 2000. The victory was made even more impressive by the fact that Brumley was a late replacement. Brumley was a last minute substitute for originally scheduled opponent Nicolyn Armstrong.

Women's Boxing Page website was there to cover the event and had these glowing words in regards to Ward after only her second professional fight: ***"Vonda is 190 lbs of solid muscle. She is a delightful young lady that the audience loved. She has little body fat and is tremendously powerful. Ward is just getting into boxing and has a lot to learn, but she will definitely be heard from in the female heavyweight division, and she has the kind of personality and attitude to contribute very positively to female boxing."***

From there, Ward got her matchup against Nicolyn Armstrong. This matchup took place on March 11, 2000, at the National Guard Armory in Findlay, Ohio. It didn't take Ward long to knock Armstrong out cold, as Ward put her in away only one minute and forty-five seconds into the first round. It was a big win for Ward because it was the first of many that would come in her home state. Ward was exited to perform well in front of her hometown fans and had these words to describe the big win: ***"It was a great feeling to get my first win in Ohio because it was a chance for the fans that followed me in basketball to also follow me in a new sport. It always feels good to win and represent your home state. We trained hard and prepared very well. We just went in and took care of business."***

Her fourth straight knockout victory to start her career came on

March 24, 2000, at the UAW Hall in Parma, Ohio. Her opponent was Lana Jack, who was a seven-time Toughwoman champion who was making her pro debut. Jack proved to be a feisty competitor for Ward to have to contend with. Jack charged Ward at the bell and looked to rush the taller and better opponent into making a mistake. Ward was ready and didn't take the bait. Jack was quickly dropped by two left-right combinations from Ward. Lana Jack was served with an eight count by the referee as she tried to clear the cob webs. Jack went back to swinging wildly but was way off balance and couldn't connect with Ward. At one point, she actually fell to the canvas again. Jack rose to her feet again and continued to come right at Vonda while getting pelted with jabs and rights. A powerful right hand put Jack down for the count just fifty-two seconds into the round. The win moved Ward's record to 4 - 0.

A typical fight day for Vonda would feature sleeping in till the late hour of 7am. She would go to the gym to stretch out and just loosen up after breakfast. She would spend the rest of the afternoon hanging low and trying to relax. Once it was time to go the arena, she would listen to the music and began to focus in on her opponent; she would visual the fight in her head the way she planned it to go. The moment of intensity would truly begin when Lorenzo wrapped her hands and warmed her up.

It was what she did after warm-ups were done that truly hit home as to what kind of person Vonda is: ***"I would get my family together - along with my trainers and manager - and we would all hold hands and pray. Lorenzo would always lead the team in prayer. We would pray for everyone's safety and victory, and then it was time to go to the ring."***

Prayer is a very special part of Vonda's life. She is a religious person who finds comfort in prayer. She was raised Catholic and she currently belongs to a Christian church. She prays every day and makes it a part of her life. She prays with her partner and daughter every night before bed. She has prayed her whole life and feels that even when you're down, that is one place you can find comfort. Vonda will tell you that God is always there for you, and there is no doubt about it. Even when times aren't going the way you want them to, there is always a way for them; you just have to keep your faith, and you will be able to look back at on it one day and understand why.

On April 27, 2000, she met Genevia Buckwalter in New York at the Hammerstein Ballroom, Manhattan Center. It was an arena famous for professional wrestling events such as Monday Night Raw and ECW events. Buckwalter tried to pull a fast one by coming into the weigh-ins seven pounds lighter than the agreed upon weight for the fight. In order for the fight to go on, Ward was forced to lose weight quickly before the night before so the fight would be saved and fought at a lighter weight class.

Buckwalter became the first fighter to make it out of the first round against Ward, but Ward still won on a second round knockout. She also gave Ward an early scare when she knocked Ward down in the first round. Ward didn't panic; she knew how to respond when being down in a fight, as she explains here: ***"I knew not to panic or get down since I was a little girl and my parents got divorced and my mother and I were left with nothing. We had to fight for everything we had, and my mom worked so hard. Just to see her will and determination to keep a roof over our heads and provide a life for me helped me set my mind to doing anything in a tough situation.***

Playing for Pat Summit also helped me mentally when I got into tough situations like that in the ring. Playing for coach Summit gave me so much strength in my world. She was a great coach, and seeing what she accomplished gave me the will to compete. My mom and coach Summit gave me the strength I needed to be successful in the ring and also bounce back from a tough spot."

Ward stayed composed and began to fight her style of fight, finally finding her range by the end of the opening round. Ward stuck to the game plan in the second round and used her reach to pepper Buckwalter with jabs. The onslaught by Ward forced Buckwalter to take two standing eight counts before the referee eventually stopped the fight with 5 seconds lefts in the second round. The referee wasted no time declaring Ward the winner for the fifth straight time in her career.

Vonda Ward was pushed to the limit for the first time in her career against Buckwalter, and was forced to overcome a knockdown. Vonda explains everything she had to go through to even allow the fight to take place, and how that affected her early stamina in the fight:" ***First of all, the night before I had to lose seven pounds because Buckhalter came to weigh-ins lighter than previously agreed. They would either cancel or I would have to lose seven pounds by morning to keep the fight scheduled. I did not want to miss the opportunity to fight in NYC, so I lost the weight by morning by running and sitting in a sauna all night. By fight time, I felt drained and very tired, but found the strength to win the fight."***

After just five fights, Ward had already earned the reputation of a knockout artist and was deeply feared within the division. She also had already earned the moniker of the "All-American Girl."

Her next fight was a first round knockout against Lisa Redding on July 17, 2000, at Station Casino in St. Charles, Missouri. Once again, it didn't take Ward long to dominate, as she put Redding away with ease by way of knockout at 31 seconds in the first round. She followed the win over Redding with another win by a second round knockout of Jeanine Tracy on August 24, 2000 in Columbus, Ohio. She stayed hot with a first round knockout against the likes of Sharon Thomas on September 23, 2000 at Packard Music Hall in Warren, Ohio. The Packard Music Hall was famous from the days of Ray Boom Boom Mancini fighting and winning there with ease.

The next knockout was of Marjorie Jones on October 19, 2000, at the Cosmopolitan in Wickliffe, Ohio. She followed that up by knocking out

Catherine Courtney.

On February 2, 2001, she met prospect Kisha Snow as part of the state fair celebrations in Columbus, Ohio. Snow came into the fight undefeated after six bouts, and she and Ward engaged in a four round war. Ward was too much for Snow, and it resulted in Snow becoming her eleventh straight knockout victim. The fight was the highlight of **ESPN2's *Friday Night Fights*.**

Snow started off the fight very aggressive by charging at the taller Ward and throwing bombs, but Ward was able to hold her off with her jab or tie her up in the early rounds, limiting the damage Snow was trying to inflict. Snow showed signs of fatigue by the end of the second round when she became more reckless, and Ward began to take advantage of the sloppy Snow and unload some very heavy blows. The strategy and patience paid off when Ward knocked Snow down in the third round and then again in the fourth round, when referee Frank Garza stopped the bout when Snow was no longer able to defend herself against the non-stop shots coming from Ward.

Vonda Ward was ecstatic with the nationally televised win over her undefeated opponent. ***"Winning my fight on national TV was such a great experience. For so many years, I watched fights on ESPN, and to have one of my fights on there was amazing. Winning on* Friday Night Fights *helped me to become a household name in women's boxing."***

Vonda Ward continued to show no signs of cooling off as she defeated Carley Pesente on June 16, 2001, at Ameristar Casino in Kansas City, Missouri in just two rounds by TKO in front of a packed and hostile crowd in Kansas City, Missouri.

Her dominance, work ethic and electric personality allowed her to become one of the pioneers in the sport. Vonda speaks about this exciting time in her career,: ***"It felt incredible to be among the top fighters in a time when the sport was just getting going. I was one of***

the pioneers. I wanted to show people that woman really can do this. Women can fight and play basketball, and l wanted to show this. It was special to be a part of the early years of women's pro basketball and women's boxing. I'm very blessed to be a part of it in my prime during those times."

She would return to Ohio for her next fight on February 22, 2002 at the Jerome Schottenstein Center in Columbus, Ohio. Fans in the crowd and media who covered it mentioned how it was the most entertaining and action-packed fight of the night, as it was live on ***ESPN Friday Night Fights***. Ward wasted little time in going on the attack and floored Jackson with a hard shot only 30 seconds into the fight. The relentless attack of Ward ended with a TKO victory over Jackson at 1:48 in the fourth round.

The hot streak and ability to put away so many opponents so quickly had everyone in the Vonda Ward camp thinking title shot, and they would soon get their wish. Vonda Ward was challenged for the IBA's world's Heavyweight title on August 16, 2002, against champion Monica McGowan. Ward would have the hometown advantage, as the fight took place in Canton, Ohio. Monica McGowan was built like a tank, weighing at 195 pounds and standing a foot shorter than the lanky Ward. She was ferocious in the ring and looked to bull her way right through the top contender.

Until that point, no fighter was able to stand with Ward and avoid getting knocked out. It led to an incredible reputation for Ward, but also led to some people questioning her stamina. Many wondered if Ward was taken deep into a fight how she would handle it.

McGowan took the fight to Ward in the early going and worked past Ward's jab with hard shots and plenty of aggression. Ward answered the challenge and began to trade with the hard-hitting McGowan. Ward was not going to back down and answered everything thrown her way. Both fighters continued to swing wildly and connect well through the first half of the fight. It was in the final four rounds that McGowan began to tire, and Ward took full advantage of the fatigued McGowan. Ward used a steady jab and continued fluid pace to keep McGowan back peddling. Ward just kept racking up the points.

Any questions about Vonda Ward's stamina were put to bed, as she dominated Monica McGowan for 10 straight rounds on her way to a decision win that allowed her to capture the IBA title. It was a unanimous decision at 99-91, 98-92, 98-92. It was a proud moment for the Northeast Ohio native, as she never let adversity stop her from reaching a dream! The fans everywhere were excited to see how her title reign would turn out. ***"Winning the IBA title was one of the most incredible feelings in my athletic career. Monica was a great fighter, and going the distance showed me that I had what it took to be a championship fighter,"*** said Ward.

It was also around this time that she decided to switch gyms, moving away from her normal camp to start training with Ed King of King's Gym. Ed knew of Vonda, but this would be the first time he had actually met and then worked with her. He recalls their first meeting in the gym and his initial impressions of her: ***"I remember being surprised at how tall she was at first. She had a very impressive stature. She came across as a very nice person, and I was happy to welcome her into the gym. I also let her know she was free to bring her clients in to train. After a little while, I began managing her, and that lasted for a good ten years. Again, her physical presence was only second to how good of person she was on the inside, as well."***

Ed goes on to explain why he feels Vonda was able to transition so well from basketball to boxing the way she did: ***"Her desire to be the best at whatever she does is really strong. No one has a stronger work ethic than Vonda. She is always trying to improve at anything she does. Her work ethic being so good is what separated her from others who tried to make the transition from sport to sport. A lot***

of people can say they want to box and then they get hit in the face and quit; Vonda just kept working hard and got better and better. Her physicality was also great, at six-foot-five-inches and about 185 pounds. Her size and incredible heart helped her become a great world champion. She never relied on just her size; she always gave heart and worked her butt off, as well."

Vonda Ward had achieved a dream goal, but quickly had to start defending the crown. In her first title defense, Ward defended her title successfully with an eighth round knockout over Kathy Rivers on December 6, 2002 at the Gund Arena in Cleveland. It was a huge crowd that packed the Gund Arena to cheer on their favorite female prize fighter. Once again, all eyes would be on Ward and Cleveland, as the bout was carried live on ESPN2's ***Friday Night Fights.***

Ward got off to a slow start and looked to be trailing through the first three rounds of the clash. It was in the fourth that she started getting the better of the hard hitting slugfest by using her reach. Ward pushed forward with a steady and sometimes an overly technique-based style, but it was working, as Ward began piling up the damage on her opponent. After several rounds of Ward having her way with Rivers and Rivers not being able to defend herself any longer, the referee stepped in and stopped it in the eighth round. Ward had these thoughts on her first title defense being a success and coming at home: ***" It was a great feeling to win a title defense at Gund Arena in Cleveland, fighting in my hometown and representing Cleveland. "***

Vonda Ward went on to defeat Martha Salazar in her next bout, this time in Las Vegas on March 1, 2003 at the Thomas and Mack Center. Martha Salazar was a late substitution for Valerie Mahfood. Salazar was unbeaten and looked to give Ward the fight of her life. The fight was set for four rounds, as the bout had been reduced from an expected six rounds to four rounds at the last moment. Despite two less rounds, it was still packed with plenty of action. Ward had been training to face

Carlette Ewell until it fell through and then Mahfood, who was unable to get away from her job as a prison guard in Texas.

Ward used her jab to perfection as Salazar struggled early to deal with the long reach. Salazar rebounded and used her strong overhand rights to connect against the steady and straight-punching Ward. At one point late in the third round, Salazar landed a heavy shot to the temple of Ward, which temporarily stunned the champion. Ward was busted up by Salazar but still came through like a champion and, once again, rose to the challenge with a split decision victory. The judges scored it 39-37, 39-37, 37-39 in favor of the champion Ward.

Vonda describes the wild situation that led to her having to face a last second replacement who weighed in at 235 pounds, a weight heavier than most heavyweight men prize fighters: ***"My fight in Vegas was supposed to be against another fighter at 175 lbs. However, she was not able to fight and we just found out the night before we were supposed to fight. The promoter brought in Martha Salazar to fight, who weighed 235 lbs. and I weighed 180 because I was contracted to fight somebody at 175 lbs. It was a tough fight, but I was determined to win even with the weight difference."***

Her next fight was a third round TKO victory over Jeanine Tracy on March 14, 2003 at Avalon Event Center in North Royalton, Ohio. This win led to a title unification bout with her familiar foe Martha Salazar. The match was held On July 11, 2003 at Memorial Civic Center in Canton, Ohio. It was a chance to face Salazar, this time with a full training camp to prepare for her.

Vonda Ward controlled the majority of the action in the rematch by boxing from the outside while the shorter, heavier Salazar tried to work inside with thunderous right crosses and left hooks. Ward used her reach and jab to score plenty of points early and often. Ward was once again tested in the fifth round when Salazar had her lone bright spot of the bout, as she landed a series of punches to the head with Ward against the ropes. Ward was able to weather the storm and went back to controlling the rest of the fight. Ward took the eight round decision on all three judges' scorecards and unified the two titles. Ward reflects on the rematch: ***"The next fight against Martha in Canton, I was much more prepared and I came to the fight at 190 lbs. I won on all cards decisively and proved I was a better fighter."***

The hot streak would be tested again finally on May 8, 2004, before 5,000 fans at the Mississippi Coast Coliseum, in Biloxi, Mississippi. Ward fought a nationally televised championship bout with Ann Wolfe. The winner would win the vacant IBA Light Heavyweight 175 lb world title. Ward wanted this title badly, and had to drop down three weight classes for a shot at the belt.

At the one minute and eight second mark of the first round, Wolfe knocked out Ward with a devastating right to the chin. Wolfe followed a vicious left hook to the body with an overhand right that caught Vonda squarely on the chin. It was a scary moment, as Ward was asleep on the mat for a few moments after the colossal blow. She was removed from the ring on a stretcher wearing a neck brace and being given oxygen, and was taken by ambulance to Gulf Coast Regional Medical Center for a CAT scan. She was diagnosed with a slight concussion. It was a double whammy for Ward, as the loss brought her undefeated streak to an end and also meant she was no longer champion. It was a bitter pill for Ward to have to swallow but, like other life lessons her life had endured, she was determined to learn and improve from it. ***"My fight with Ann Wolfe was my first loss. I went down three weight classes to challenge her for the world title. Going to a lighter weight class and losing that weight was probably not the right decision, but I don't use it as an excuse. Ann Wolfe was a great fighter and caught me with an overhand right that won her the fight. I decided to use it as a learning experience and improve as a fighter. Any time you lose or experience a setback in life or in sports, it is an opportunity to grow and improve and become a better person or athlete. Lessons***

I've learned in my life and competitive nature helped to become a champion. There are two women in my life who have shown me how to be successful in sports and in life: my mom and Pat Summitt."

Not one to stay down long, Vonda Ward bounced back quickly. On December 10, 2004, at the Gund Arena in Cleveland, Ohio, Ward returned to the boxing ring, knocking out Canadian born Marsha Valley in four rounds in Cleveland. Valley was knocked down twice in the fourth round before the fight was stopped. It was vintage Ward, as she used a constant jab effectively to set up power combinations. Ward explains why she was able to bounce back from the loss and rebound with such a solid victory that evening: ***"I was able to be so successful because of my determination and natural athletic abilities."***

Four months later on April 29, 2005 at the Wolstein Center in Cleveland, Ohio, Vonda retained her IBA Heavyweight title by stopping Elizabeth Kerin in the second round of their title fight. The win didn't come without adversity, however, as Vonda was knocked down by Kerin's first right hand of the first round and struggled to get back to her feet, barely beating the count. It was a watershed moment for Ward because she showed that she could suffer an early brutal knockdown and bounce back. It is the true test of a fighter after they suffer their first real knockout - as Ward did against Wolfe - to be able to come back from that and not let future knockdowns keep them down. Ward proved her chin was as strong as ever and put away any demons that may have been following her after the loss to Wolfe.

The back to back wins were good enough to put her back in title contention and on July 15, 2005, at the Gund Arena in Cleveland, Ohio, Ward was granted an IBA Cruiserweight Title Shot against Cassandra Geigger. Ward was victorious, as she won the 10 round decision and took home the title. The fight nearly ended late in the seventh round when a series of punches forced Geiggar to one knee, and she got up after the 8-count from referee Jim Villers. Geiggar managed to hang on to finish the fight, but it was dominated by Ward from start to finish.

Following the title win, her next fight was once again against Martha Salazar, a majority decision victory scored in favor of Ward at 97-93, 97-93, 95-95 on February 10, 2007, at the Wolstein Center in Cleveland, Ohio. The win also brought Ward the WBC and WIBA Heavyweight championship belts.

Her final fight of her glamorous and legendary pro career came on February 23, 2008 at Chapparells Community Center in Akron, Ohio, against Carlette Ewell. She was once again victorious with a 10 round unanimous decision. The judges scored it 100-90, 100-90, 99-91 in favor of Ward.

Her pro career finished with a record of 23 - 1 with 17 KO's. She will go down as one of the greatest athletes in the history of women's athletics. It didn't always come easy for Ward, but she was never afraid to work hard and sacrifice. She had these final words on her wonderful career and prestigious legacy:***" I feel blessed to have represented northeast Ohio in basketball and in boxing. We have so many great athletes that come out of northeast Ohio, and to be amongst them is an honor. I want to thank all of my fans for their support throughout all of the years. Keep supporting our athletes from northeast Ohio.***

The sincere love and support I get from people today after being retired makes me feel good inside. I 'm not in the papers anymore and I'm just living a regular everyday life, but it is still nice to meet fans who show respect and make me feel good for what I accomplished."

Vonda Ward is not only an intimidating women on the court and in the ring, but she is a beautiful women outside of it, as well. Many women would kill for her looks: tall, blonde and an incredibly in-shape figure. She could have easily went into modeling or broadcasting when her in-ring career was done, she possessed every skill needed to do so. Once again, however, she showed her class instead and decided to give back to the sport in one of the most unselfish ways possible: she chose to train people instead and help them improve their lives at King's Gym.

Vonda explains her reasons to stay out of the lime light and instead focus on helping others with their careers, as well as training non-fighters just improve their overall lives: ***"I always have been interested in the training part of sports. I wanted to train people in general for health and wellness. I have always wanted to help people and give back to people, and this is a great way to do it as far as the health industry goes. It is a great job because I get to help people physically but also mentally. It is not just looking good, it is feeling good mentally. It is rewarding in a lot of different ways."***

Not only was Vonda a champion in the ring, but out of the ring as well, as her true character showed time and time again when it came to helping others. Once a year, she runs a Toys for Tots campaign at King's Gym where she usually collects so many toys for charity that it takes two truckloads to pick them all up.

Vonda also helps with the Emergency Relief Agency out of Macedonia, Ohio. This is an organization that helps with families going through hardships and tragedies. They help families in any situation, and Vonda was a perfect fit to help with such a great cause. A month doesn't go by that Vonda and King's Gym aren't donating something to a worthy organization. She has helped with everything from the American Cancer Society to the Red Cross.

Perhaps one of the most sincere and impressive things Vonda Ward did once again did not happen in the ring, but outside of it. During Hurricane Katrina - despite it being in the middle of her second title run - she took time out to gather supplies for the victims, rent a truck and then drove the supplies down there herself. She filled up a semi-truck within three days to drive down.

Vonda explains why it is so important for her to give back: ***"It is very important to give back, even when you are in a position where you don't have a lot to give. If you have the name recognition as a***

professional athlete, then you can use it to raise money for charity. Even if you can only bring awareness, you should, because that means more money and people bringing help. "

With her boxing career behind her, she continues to give back to the sport that has given so much to her. She is now a head trainer and co-promoter of fights out of the famed "King's Gym" in Northeast Ohio. She has become one of Ed King's closest co-workers and friends over the years, as she has once again made a smooth transition, this time from active competitor to trainer.

Ed explains why she has been able to become a wonderful trainer in the gym: ***"Her work ethic is superior and she has a general concern for people. She always wants the best for her clients and wants them to have wellness in their lives. It isn't about money for her or just counting reps, it is about truly helping people. She makes sure that each client everyday truly gets the total experience. It is her caring, and I think that separates her. She always wants to her client be the best they can be, and that doesn't just mean as a fighter. She still has a level of intensity with whatever the client wants from her, even if they don't want to step foot in a ring and just train for the fitness aspect. She treats them well and helps them in that particular way, as well. She does a lot to bring wellness into the lives of anyone she trains, and that goes back to her being so sincere. She truly wants her clients to be the best they can be. Plus, she is a former World Champion, and how many gyms can say they have a former World Champ training young fighters?"***

Perhaps the biggest honor of Vonda's life is being a mother to a thirty-month old daughter. She makes time for her daughter and is a proud mother; being raised from a great one has helped set the example for Vonda. She touched on how important it is to be a good mother: ***"I have always wanted to be a mother, but being a professional athlete I had to put that on hold for a while. I was finally able to seriously pursue***

that. It is such a blessing to be a mother. It is a great experience, and having a child is a true miracle. We never gave up after trying for four years, and now we have her and it is a blessing!"

The Vonda Ward that I have been blessed to know is the woman who would do anything for the right cause, and someone who has worked her heart out and her butt off her whole life to be the best she could be. In a day and age where so many athletes are concerned with their "legacy," Vonda Ward's main concern has always been being a good person who lived her life by the golden rule. She is the picture of class and respect. She never stopped working hard, and never stopped giving back. For every little girl out there with a Lady Gaga or Beyoncé poster on their wall, I truly hope there is one with a Vonda Ward poster, as well. She is the role model this world needs for its children and young athletes. Vonda Ward is a warrior, a champion and truly a woman who lives every day of her life to inspire!

Epilogue

It was December 29, 2005, and I was at a Greek Orthodox Church for a wedding. It was unique because I'm Roman Catholic, and it was my first exposure to something that different in the realm of religion. It was an interesting time in my life to say the least. At 23 years old, I didn't have much going on for myself. I was working full time at Heinen's Grocery store as a stock boy, but only made $7.45 an hour. Clearly on a salary so low, I couldn't afford to move out of my parent's house just yet, and I felt like a total loser. I even worked one day a week delivering wine on one of my two off days from Heinen's, but it wasn't enough. Every single day, I dreamt of moving out, one day writing a book and having my own family. On many days, it seemed like those things would never happen.

My date that night was a girl named Polly; I was in love with her. We had met the prior June and despite the fact that she was leaving for the military in January 2006, I let myself fall for her. I knew the whole time she would be leaving for the Air Force, and I also knew she had a significant other in New York that she saw once every couple of months. I couldn't help it; I was smitten with what I couldn't have.

It was a point in the night when they called for a couple's dance during the reception, and we shared what would be our last slow dance together. I couldn't take it any longer, so I took a walk. As I was walking in the back of the church that was connected to the ballroom reception hall, I began to cry. I simply lost it. I thought about Polly leaving, I thought about dying alone and I thought about never getting a chance in life that despite my hard work just never seemed to come along.

It was at that moment of great despair that I felt a heavy hand on my shoulder and heard the words, ***"what troubles you, my son?"*** I looked up at this man, who was at least 6 foot 6 inches if not taller - well over a foot taller than me. It was a Presbyter, or in terms I was used too, a priest. It was incredible because I didn't see the man; I have no idea where he came from, and all of a sudden he was just there.

I briefly told him that my biggest fear in life was dying alone, and that I thought I was living a life of a loser with no future. He told me to close my eyes, bow my head and then lean back. I did what I was told and laid back in his arms as he dipped my head under a pool of water in the nearby baptism fountain. He said a prayer in a language I couldn't understand, lifted me back up then walked away singing. I dried off then looked around to see if anyone had seen it. No one did; I was completely alone.

Over the next 10 years, my life would change drastically. Shortly after Polly left, my eyes were wide open, and I was lucky enough to meet my future wife, Emily. Meeting Emily changed everything for me; it turned my life around. I soon got a better job, moved out, starting writing my first book *Hero*, and began to grab life by the horns. Emily and I got married in August 2011, and two years later we had our first child, a beautiful daughter named Margaret, and we have never been happier.

This is why I would urge anyone to never give up on your dreams and to believe that with hard work and prayer anything is possible. The stories of the Venesile family, Cathy Wade, Chuck Galeti, my mother Maria DeLuca McKee, Vonda Ward and the Kunes Family have proven that. It is never too late to change your stars and no matter what the odds are or the obstacles put in your life, they are never large enough to not be overcome.

I was honored to be able to tell these stories, because they can help anyone in any walk of life. We never know the challenges that await us behind each door in life. Noah was a 9 years old with the strength and courage of 90 men. Maria refused to listen to the doctors and never stopped achieving her dreams, no matter how much pain she had to go through to get there. Vonda Ward's injury would have retired most athletes; instead, she used it to transition into a career and now is helping every life she touches. Chuck Galeti went from finding the bottom of an empty bottle to finding Christ. Cathy Wade and John Venesile turned a death sentence into a second chance at life. None of these warriors ever gave up, they just kept fighting and providing inspiration for anyone who heard of their tale.

We are all better for hearing these stories. It puts things in perspective and allows us to be grateful for some of the simple pleasures God has put in our lives. The next time you see a group of kids playing in the yard, stop and smile, because for Noah, he almost never had that chance again. If you're around a person who goes into a seizure, don't be scared, know that you are there because God wants you to help that person. At a bar and someone is making an ass out of themselves, don't judge, offer to buy them some coffee; sometimes a drunk is just a lonely scared person crying out for help.

What we see and what the real story is can be miles apart. This isn't sports where things are judged on points and goals, it is real life where a hero can be around every corner. In the end we can only play the cards dealt to us. It doesn't mean we have to fold, however; it just means we have our own chance to defy the odds and live every single day to inspire!

CPSIA information can be obtained at www.ICGtesting.com
Printed in the USA
BVOW06s1243090516

447340BV00019B/105/P